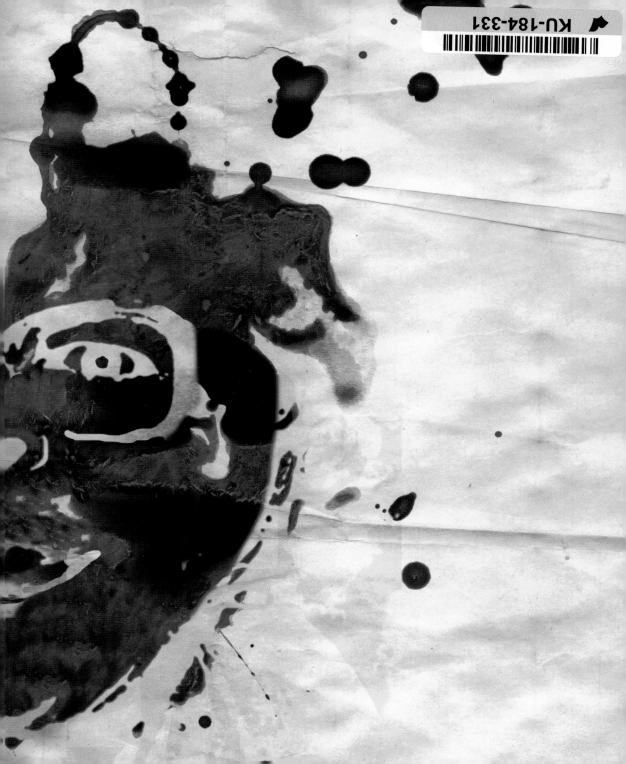

MY NAME IS TUBBS

I like to find things.
When I am out on the
moors burying people with
my husband, Edward, I
offen find things. Shiny things or things of intrest. Edward
tells me not to pick them up, especially the brown ones, but I
allways do, and I bring them back to my secret den where Edward
doesn't know about. Hee hee hee hee hee hee hee hee hee hee-
heeeee. Hee hee heeee he. Hee. Heh. Oh dear me. Edward would
kill me if he found out I am actually making a BOOK of these
things, but one day when I finnish it I am going to give it to
him as a supprise.

Edward doesn't know that I learned my reading and writing yet! I
did this by finding some books from a place called school, where
Janet and John live, with Spot. Spot goes to the farm. John goes
with him. New word: farm. J'ai trouvee aussi les livres de Pierre
et Marianne, qui habitent avec xavier. Xavier va la ferme. But I
like Spot the most best. What was that? No. Nothing. I thought I
heard something. Hhhhmmm. I'm going to sleep now anyway.

Now I am awake. That's better. Just move round here a bit. Yes.
I like the taste of yellow food that comes from my eyes when I
have been asleep. Nice. You will see from my book that I do not
throw anything away, I like to keep things and look at them. I
am keen on local history, and one day I hope to write a book
about it. You can learn a lot of things about people by what
they throw away, as you will see from my book.

EDWARD

my love

Edward and I were childhood sweethearts, and
I cannot ever remember a time we were not
destined to be wedded. (There was the time
when grandpa said he wanted to marry me, but
grandma was still alive. Otherwise who
knows!) Edward is a very clever man and
knows more things about the world than I do.
He was in a war, and I feared for his life,
but he returned looking even more radiant
than ever, even though his skin had gone
brown. He was awarded some medals for bravery. I will make a mirror-baby of them
later, I'm sure he wont mind if I "borrow"
them. Hee hee hee hee hee hee hee hee
heeeeeheeee! Naughty Tubbs.

These are not mirrors! They come from the flashbox,
which was my first good "find". A man came to the
shop to buy I can I can't. He was not a Local man,
so Edward burned him. But in his coat I found this
machine, and when I pressed the button it winked at
me and had a baby, which looked just like me (see
above). Edward said it was a devil-box and would take
my name to hell.

Then I made a mirror of Edward and he liked his baby,
so we decided to keep it. Since then the machine has
made many babies for us, which is nice of it, because
my insides are all wrong.

MY FAMILY TRUNK

This is my family trunk. The last name is of my darling son and nephew David. I cannot hope to provide David with a little bride for the time being, so this is where the line may end. I hope David might meet a nice local no-tail and we can add a branch onto our family trunk.

Edward Trubbs

David

Farthing Wood

MARVIN MEDIUM

Pyramid of Fear

Temple Of Doom

Mong

Royston Vasey

Peggy Mount

TON PLACE

STEPHEN STREET

OXFORD STREET

DENNY LANE

PENNY LANE

CLEO LANE

CHARING CROSS ROAD

LEICESTER SQUARE

TATTOO CLOSE

The Great Intelligence

Acker Bilk

Two Ton Tessie

Mrs. Mills

St. Mary Of Bethlhem Hospital

We did not burn these ones

Royston Vasey Town Hall
Royston Vasey

Tel:
Fax:
E-n
ISD

Dear Friends,

How the fuck are you? I am fine thank you. This is Mayor Larry Vaughn. The first citizen of Royston Vasey. That makes me the biggest cunt in the place.

We have compiled this beautiful brochure in order to arouse your interest (not unlike the tit mags Pop keeps behind his copies of Total Film) and maybe encourage you to bring your business to Royston Vasey. Many small businesses already thrive here - just ask Nicole who can always be found hanging around outside Burger Me after dark. (She s a lovely lass with a fine pair of milk-shooters and can take it right down to the tonsils if you know what I mean gents.) Anyway back to this shitting brochure. It was a bastard to bring off I can tell you - like me after a Friday night session in the Monkey s Paw - you ask my missus.

At present our little town is only small - like a Chinaman s cock. But we hope to make it much larger - as Nicole said when she shoved three fingers up my arsehole.

So come to Royston Vasey! I can promise you a bloody good time, pardon my French.

Yours sincerely

Larry Vaughn (Mayor)

ROYSTON VASEY

"Once Discovered, Never Forgotten"

The town is first
dix to the Dom
referred to as ':
outside'. From these h
town grew and grew u
teenth century Poll Ta
'two huttes with a pig.

Throughout the f
into the sixteen
further until a h
into its pair of huts. L
time centred on pig's
Knuckle-Scrape – a ki
porcine filth.

Th
18th
nals
wend

Th
Vaseye
ty but
for mo
saries
the to
as tho
an bro
her ha

Set amidst the gentle rolling hills of the
Vale of Tiers, known for its equable
weather and mediterranean ambience–
Royston Vasey is a town like no other.

Twinned with
Duisburg

Well served by modern road and rail connections Royston Vasey is a bustling, happy **community full of fascinating** history and colourful sights.

Then, in 1642, like every other community in England, civil war came to Royston Vasey. After suffering endless, pointless attempts to grow wool on them, the pigs rose up against their cruel human masters. Setting up an animal's republic with other dissatisfied creatures including otters, bears and silverfish, their insurrection was eventually overcome when they were simply rounded up in a barn and set on fire.

X ...entioned in an appen- ...day Book, where it is ...hutte with a pigge ...mble beginnings the ...til in the mid-four- ...records refer to it as ...: outside.'

...teenth century and ..., the settlement grew ...ndred people crowded ...al industry at that ...vool, together with ...d of jam derived from

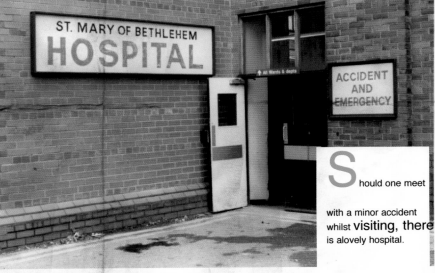

Should one meet with a minor accident whilst **visiting, there** is a lovely hospital.

A short time after this, Royston Vasey played host to a tribe of American Indians – the Nick Nacks. They had arrived from the New World with the town's very own founding fathers who, disenchanted, had returned after only a week in their ship The Woolly Pig. Keen to foster relations with the mysterious newcomers the townsfolk robbed and killed the Nick Nacks before burying them in quicklime. Indeed much of modern day Royston Vasey is built on this, the only Red Indian Burial Ground in Britain.

Royston Vasey
Chronicle

18 HIGH STREET WEST, ROYSTON VASEY, RV1 5SF
incorporating the **High R**
Advertising: 0016 2010209   Editorial: 0016 0034917   E-mail: localnews@localpeople.co.u

BUTCHER GOTCHA!

• We'll "meat" again - local police aim to track down fly-by-night butcher, Hilary Briss.

by WAYNE GACY

POLICE ARE STILL looking for prominent Royston Vasey Butcher Hilary Briss, 52, after a daring dawn raid, led to the arrest of local magistrate Maurice Evans, and Councillor Samuel Chignell.

Story continues on page 8.

• Right- Shamed local businessmen lead away yesterday.
• Below- Briss had been under observation for some time.

'MURDER', SHE HOPED

MEMBERS OF ROYSTON Vasey Conservative Club will tomorrow night witness three grisly murders and will then be asked 'Whodunnit' by a high-profile Police Inspector from Scotland Yard. But the victims and police will all be **ACTORS** performing this Murder Mystery as an after-dinner **ENTERTAINMENT.**

As well as being asked to 'play detective', guests will be treated to a 3-course meal, including coffee and mince, and will each be given a 'clue-pack' and a 'crime sheet' which they can take home, frame, or show to friends.

"I think this could be the next big craze," said Ailsa Manning, who has collected together the actors under the name Bloody Puddings to perform the show. "I remember when they started with round tea bags here a couple of years ago, everyone mocked it. Now they all bloody drink them."

Ailsa, a former nurse and child prostitute, got the idea from a friend who once went to London. "She came back saying it was all the rage there. And I've heard tell of one in Preston. So I thought 'Why not here?' "

Ailsa wrote the 'script' for Blue Murder in one twenty minute sitting. The 'action' takes place in a 1920's Paris Club called Nana's, and tells of a glamorous cabaret girl Fifi La Threlfall who wants to get to the top by whatever means possible.

So does that make Fifi a suspect? Can-can she make it to La Moulin Rouge? Ah, you'll have to wait and see! Ailsa is keeping tight-lipped for now, but promised blood, guts and a selection of cold starters for just £29.99.

"It's bloody good fun and them as don't like it can just fuck off," she trilled.

Paws For Thought!

Royston Vasey's Own Canine Impresario speaks!

World-famous canine film fanatic Kenny Harris has a treat in store for his dedicated customers. Kenny, 56, owner of the Kenny Harris Dog Cinema on Denny Lane is offering a special 'in season' ticket for this spring's line up of doggy delights.

'We have some real treats for everyone from the satirical brilliance of Tom Ropelewski's Look Who's Talking Now – fantastic voice work from Danny DeVito and Diane Keaton – to the light-hearted magic of Norman Tokar's The Ugly Dachshund.

'Everyone had better hurry up and get their 'paws' on a ticket or they'll be on heat with anticipation!'

So what does Kenny see as the highlight of his new season?

'Oh it's definitely going to be the 'Late 80's/Early 90's Dog Renaissance weekend April 7th/8th. Many true dog film fans had given up on the idea that the

• Beyond our Ken! There's no wuff justice for this regular at Kenny Harris's Dog Cinema yesterday.

Hollywood dream factory would ever again give us a truly great canine caper but the twilight of the twentieth century proved to be an Indian summer of mutt-tastic movies. We've got probably the Rolls Royce of all dog/cop movies Turner and Hooch – Hanks got all the glory but I reckon Beasley as Hooch deserved the laurels. Then there's Beethoven, Beethoven's Second and best of all a double bill of K9 and K9000. There are those who believe the latter two movies are related but whilst they both share a narcotics-based plotline – they couldn't be more different. One has a robot dog, the other a german shepherd.

And has Kenny ever considered diversifying into, say, cat movies. 'Absolutely not,' he says firmly. I had a woman from Neggercook writing to me asking just that. She'd seen That Darn Cat on holiday in Brisbane and wanted it on for her nephew who was Down's. But I told her 'on no account'. Cat films are rubbish. Everyone knows that. There's nowt to 'em. People say to me, Kenny, that The Cat From Outer Space – that's a good cat film. It's not. Aristocats. Hateful. What were Disney thinking of after the majesty of 101 Dalmations? I hate cats. I worked as a colliery engineer for fifteen years and wild cats gathered in the shaft beneath the lift drop. They'd swarm round your ankles as you descended into the seams. The whiskers are the worse. Like fuse-wire run through their cheeks.

I've heard there's a man in Sorehole who's got a collection of cat videos who'll run off copies for people. But at the Kenny Harris Dog Cinema, no way!'

Well Kenny's certainly 'dog'-matic about that one!

BRIEFLY...

FOUNDER OF DEAF CHESS DIES

A Royston Vasey man who made a huge difference to the lives of deaf people has died following a brave battle against headaches. Wilfred Dunwell of Pollock Road died aged 89 at St. Mary's of Bethlehem Hospital on Wednesday (12th). Mr Dunwell founded the U.K.'s first Deaf Chess Club with his wife Kathleen 25 years ago. This proved a struggle due to ignorance about the deaf.

Club member June Keeble said "It wasn't always easy going, but his big achievement was when he managed to get deaf people to play against those with full hearing."

Deaf chess operates through a system of hand-signals from voluntary helpers, and guide rails. Since its creation with just 6 members, the club has gone from strength to strength and now has 7 members who meet twice a year.

Current Deaf Chess champ Gregory "The Bishop" Mawl, said yesterday "I knew Wilf Dunwell for over 10 years and I never heard a word said about him."

Mr Dunwell leaves behind a wife, Kathleen, who he described as 'my black queen', and four white pawns. The funeral was quiet.

VASEY GIRLS JIG CHAMPS

Hidden away in the depths of Royston Vasey are two champion jig dancers. Shasta Books (15) and her sister Kellie (56) of Nazareth Avenue, have been jigging since the age of five.

Proud mum Carey said "They love jigging. They love to jig," despite fierce competition, they were picked to jig for a Scandinavian jigging tour, where they won in the Best Jigging and Best New Jig categories respectively.

Dear Bernice...

...If you need the advice of a sympathetic friend, the Reverend Bernice Woodall has all the answers.

Star Letter

A CARPET OF OLD WHITE DOG EGGS

Dear Bernice

I have always been very fond of animals but none have ever been as important to me as my Corgi Bitch called copper. A few weeks ago she was clipped by a car and the vet says she can't last much longer. My other pets are upset too. How will I ever get over losing her?

S.Smith, Tontonmacute

Bernice replies...

You say you have lots of other animals. I bet your house stinks. I can well imagine the state of the place. Fur everywhere, overflowing litter trays. If you're in there for five minutes you'd be scratching your skin raw for days. I bet you're one of those scary old women you see walking around dragging a gang of sick strays with her cos she's too soppy to have them put down. I heard about this woman once who was a retired vet. The neighbours complained about the stink and when they got there the place was a foot deep in old dog eggs. There's mebbe sixty wild dogs in there. A pair of them had taken over the whole staircase and the others were so interbred they were scarcely dogs at all. Is that what your house is like, miss? They say people come to resemble their animals you must look like the Thing.

PUT IT OUT OF ITS MISERY

Dear Bernice

Our son was born quadriplegic. Although his disability is severe we love him dearly and were prepared to try anything the doctors might suggest to improve his condition. They performed spinal surgery but unfortunately there were complications and he suffered irreparable brain damage leaving him both blind and deaf. Although we are both practising Christians we are seriously considering taking Michael's life. We are at the end of our tether. Please help.

Anon

Bernice replies...

First of all can I say I think it's very nice that you've given it a name. Now, my heart goes out to this poor couple and their ruined progeny. What should they do? Well nobody's talking about wrapping the poor bairn in a bin bag and chucking him in the canal. No, in this day and age it's just as simple to administer a lethal injection. And there are other cases where similar measures might apply. If you've an ugly daughter, perhaps, or a son born ginger, a syringe full of diamorphine might just do the trick. It's like these girls I see outside my window, sitting on the bollards outside Victoria Wine with one bottle of Hooch between them, talking about boys till nine or ten o'clock at night. If I had my way I'd get one of them back to my flat and turn my hairdryer full heat onto her tummy and privates. That would teach 'em to stop riding their bikes two abreast on the pavement when I'm struggling back with my shopping.

MY SPECIAL HELPLINE

If you need advice through a difficult or troubled time, my recorded messages are here to help.

If you would like to contact Bernice about any problems you might be experiencing, write to her here, at the Chronicle. The sender of the most distressing letter wins a £5 book token.

Little Don Returns With New Venture

POPULAR LOCAL ENTREPRENEUR

Little Don is making a dramatic comeback after his previous venture was destroyed by vandals who have yet to be caught. 'I was very upset,' says Don who now lives in a large shed at the bottom of his brother in law's garden. 'The Roundabout Zoo was a nice little earner, you know. People would come from all over to see it. The chimp was the most popular. A little girl wrote him a postcard once.'
Little Don's animals were stolen by person or persons unknown, leaving his urban menagerie empty of exhibits. His brother-in-law, Eddie Cantor, takes up the story: 'Don were devastated. He were a broken man. Those animals were like children to him. I saw him feeding the goat with a spoon once.' It was Cantor who had provided Don with Pickles the Chimpanzee. 'I called in a favour with a Ringmaster friend. But I couldn't get another. They're like gold dust. So I let Don have the s h e d .'
But Little Don is unbowed by tragedy. He is about to launch a venture that he hopes will prove every bit as popular as his traffic-bound menagerie.

'It's on a smaller scale, you know. People can't expect me to pluck something out of nowhere. Critics might say it's a mere novelty but I think the kid's'll like it.' Billed simply as 'Little Don's Shoebox Circus' the pint-size arena is actually fashioned out of an old s h o e b o x . 'I was lying in the shed one morning feeling very down. I was wondering what was left for me. Then I saw the box on a shelf next to some old Growbags. It got me thinking. I'd thought before, 'I can't get the animals, I can't get the animals', but then I realised that weren't true.' The exhibits include a mole, a snail and a moth. 'The moth is one of those big furry ones that look like they're wearing a jumper. I tied some cotton to it so it doesn't go wild and upset the mole. For 50p people can come round and have a look'.

LOCAL MAN LINES POCKETS

AN UNIMAGINA-TIVE, EXPLOITA-TIVE, failed journalist has hit upon a winning way of earning cash. Robin Bastard of Backbottoms, Royston Vasey is a big fan of cult BBC2 comedy The Porn Dwarves which uses the town as the setting for the fictional town of Boothby Graffoe. 'I hadn't watched the show and wasn't even aware it was filming in Vasey until a friend told me about it. All my other schemes had failed so I thought I'd scavenge off other people's hard work and initiative.'
The macabre show features a clown with leprosy, a baker who sells bread made of polystyrene and the terrifying Derek Twins with their popular catchphrase 'I wrote that!' amongst others.
Robin, who until recently was working in a morgue, hit upon the idea of printing T shirts and other memorabilia. He also created a website devoted to the show. 'I thought I'd get in fast before the BBC knew what was going on. Why should I fucking care? It's a bit of money isn't it?'
The Porn Dwarves themselves were unavailable for comment but a BBC spokesman said they were considering chipping in a grand each to have Robin, and other parasitic cunts like him, knocked off.

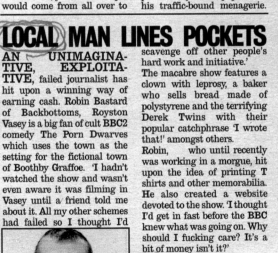

• 'parasitic cunt', Robin Bastard was unavailable for comment yesterday.

Daffy Dads Competition!!!

We asked for your paintings and drawings of some of the crazy things your Dad gets up to. As usual we had a torrent of entries. This month's winner is 11-year-old Matthew Corrigan from Lovecrafty.

Says Matthew: "Dad's a real laugh. He often has us in stitches." He wins a £10 book token.

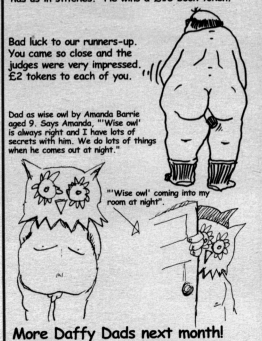

Bad luck to our runners-up. You came so close and the judges were very impressed. £2 tokens to each of you.

Dad as wise owl by Amanda Barrie aged 9. Says Amanda, "'Wise owl' is always right and I have lots of secrets with him. We do lots of things when he comes out at night."

"'Wise owl' coming into my room at night".

More Daffy Dads next month!

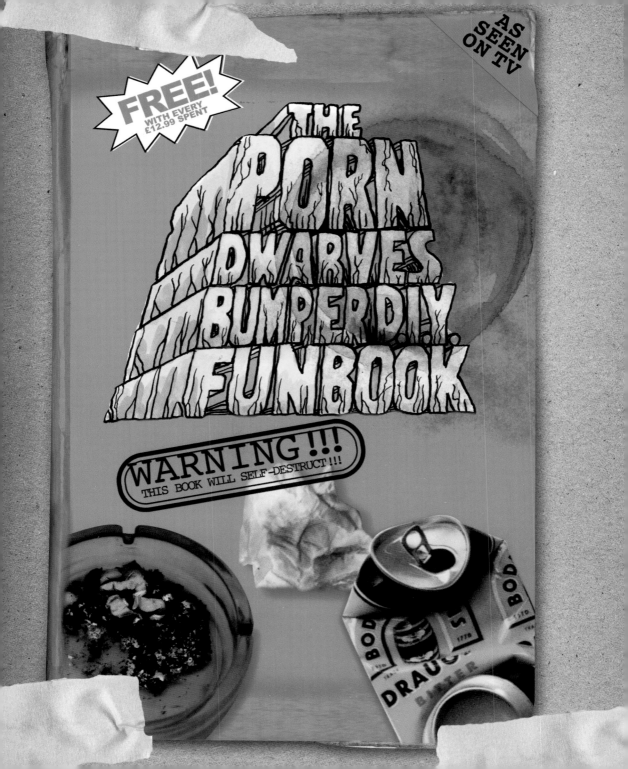

-HA!!! HA-HA!!! HA-HA!!! HA-HA!!

THIS BOOK BELONGS TO...

Saddam Hussain

TONY BLAIR (age 6)

DES O' CONNOR

Mother Thereza

THE PORN DWARVES WOULD LIKE TO THANK...

Andy (cut and paste) Miller, Clive Priddle and Rachel Connolly at Fourth Estate.

Philippa Baile, Nicola Hammond, Tony Lyons, Kate Stretton and Duncan Youel at M2 and Phil Healey at Planet X for design and art direction (skin kindly donated by Mike Plumb).

Yves Barre, Helen Barrett, Steve Bendelack, Colette Blair, Roy 'Chubby' Brown, Chiggy and all at PBJ Management, Frances Cox, Pete Edwards, Don Estelle, Paul Hayes-Marshall, Grenville Horner, Sarah Kane, Rob Kitzman, Ted Robbins, Jemma Rodgers, Rudolf Rocker, Sarah Smith, Joby Talbot, Bridget Thornborrow, Nick West, Vanessa White, Jane, and Robert Woodall.

And special thanks to all the people of Royston Vasey. May you never leave.

A Local Book For Local People - The League Of Gentlemen

First published in Great Britain in 2000 by Fourth Estate Limited, 6 Salem Road, London W2 4BU

Text copyright © Jeremy Dyson, Mark Gatiss, Steve Pemberton and Reece Shearsmith

All photographs copyright © The League Of Gentlemen, unless otherwise stated.

Photographs, page 69 copyright © Reuters - Popperfoto, page 116 copyright © Fatih Saribas - Reuters - Popperfoto.

The right of Jeremy Dyson, Mark Gatiss, Steve Pemberton and Reece Shearsmith to be identified as the authors of this work has been asserted by them in accordance with the Copyright, Design and Patents Act 1988.

Designed by Planet X / M2

ISBN 1-84115-346-X. Printed in Italy

IA-HA!!! HA-HA!!! HA-HA!!! HA-HA!!!

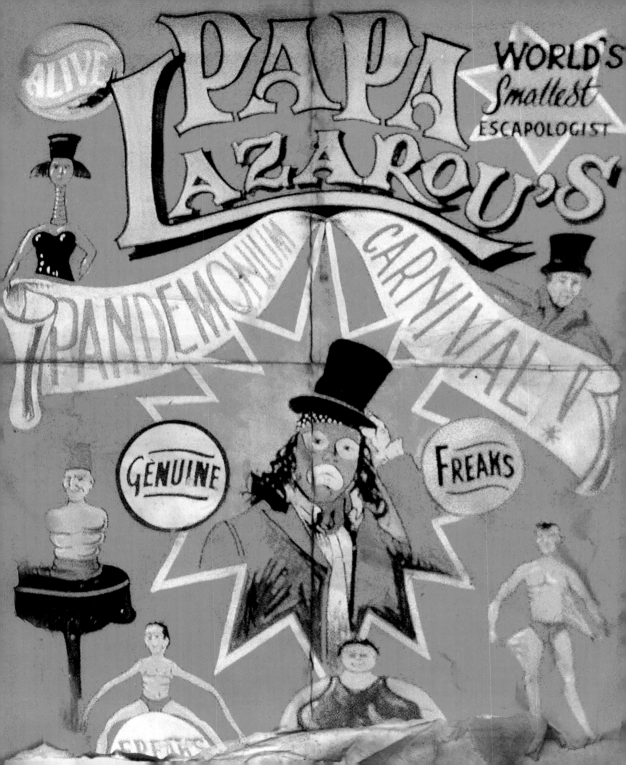

HELLO DAVE. WANNA SEE SOMETHING SCARY DAVE? THEN WHY NOT PAY ME A VISIT AT

PAPA LAZAROU'S

★ ★ ★ ★   ★ ★ ★ ★

PANDEMONIUM CARNIVAL

WE HAVE MANY FREAKS HERE. **BELONGING TO YOU.** IF YOU GIVE ME A RING* I WILL INTRODUCE YOU TO THEM:

MAMA LAZAROU

MY WIFE CAN READ YOUR FORTUNEBYLOOKINGIN YOUR TOILET DAVE

PASSI

THE BEARDED LADY. I CAUGHT HER IN DARKEST BORNEO. SHE'S MY WIFE NOW

SIMBA
PEBBLE & TIK-TIK

THESE ARE NOT CHILDREN **DAVE, THEY ARE MONSTERS. SEE FOR YOUR SELF**

LE TERRIBLE ENFANT
OISSEAU

PART BOY, PART BIRD. I WON HIM FROM A VOO-DOO CHIEF IN AFRICA. HE TRIED TO FLY AWAY SO I BROKE HIS WINGS

SPECIAL SHOW!! I CAN FORCE ALL OF THESE CURSED CREATURES TO STRIP BARE AND DANCE FOR YOU UP CLOSE IN THE MOST DREADFUL SPECTACLE I CALL...

THE FULL MONSTER

PLUS: WIN A GOLDFISH, GUESS THE GIANT'S WEIGHT, BUY SOME PEGS DAVE.
*AUTOSM SPRAU KANA TIKPANA SAN DUOR BU NO SARASMEEY

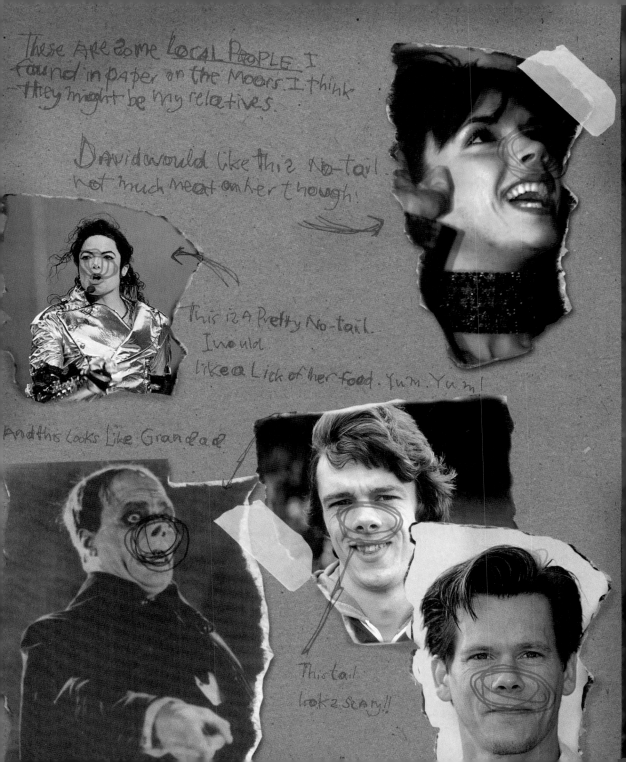

These Are some LOCAL PEOPLE I
found in paper on the Moors. I think
they might be my relatives.

David would like this No-tail.
Not much meat on her though!

This is A Pretty No-tail.
I would
like a Lick of her food. Yum Yum!

And this looks Like Grandad

This tail
looks scary!!

I have only ever loved an angel
by Hilary Briss, High-Class Butcher

It is midnight now. Soon they will come for me, I am sure of it. I do not have long to write these few words, but write them I will. I want the world to know. About her. About her beauty. About her calm, measured company in times of crisis. Her sagacity and tenderness. And her udders. Christ her udders.

I have done so many bad things.

She wasn't the first Mrs. Briss. But the others meant nothing to me. Cheap. Worthless. Dissatisfying. Like a bit of scrag end. They started well. But then they turned. They always turn.

Winnie was different

When did I first meet her? Is it only four years ago? The Great Yorkshire Show. Blazing hot. The smell of straw. I was looking for somewhere to go. There'd been an ugly incident with a lady urinating extravagantly in the Gents. At that time Winnie was stepping out with a fellah with whom I was on nodding terms. Old Jed Tinsel. He was whispering something in her ear. But I know she had no interest in him.

She looked straight at me with those liquid brown eyes – like two big, fresh kidneys. I suddenly felt alive, as though my body was on fire. I just prayed to God that I wouldn't do it again. I wouldn't. I musn't…

Our first conversation was polite enough. Formal. I asked her about her yield. But she was shy – Tinsel answered for her. Said she'd not yet calved. That was it. She was unbroken. In that moment I knew I must have her.

She must have known what was in my mind, for she batted her lashes coquettishly. And although she had never known a man I vowed that soon she would. Aye!

I talked terms with Farmer Tinsel there and then but the rogue would have none of it. He is an uncouth man. Giblets in the great scheme of things. It was right that I should take her. Tinsel went off to the beer tent leaving us alone. I asked her what she thought of him. Her tail went up vertical and she shat. I needed no other encouragement.

That night, the night I took her, was moonless. I stole across the field where the brute was keeping her. Thought I heard a voice behind me. But it was only one of Tinsel's scarecrows. Quickly I untied her bonds. Never will I forget that journey home. The terror of discovery. The heat of anticipation. The clop of her hooves on the road. I felt like Jack in Jack and the Beanstalk but not the same. No magic beans would take her away from me.

Oh my love, my love, maybe it is a good thing I will have to leave. The clock is ticking. It has begun again and it might have finished you. Like the others. I am sorry. So sorry.

Oh my love those were the golden days. Little runs out on other moonless nights. Sharing a joke, cosy evenings by the fire, stuffing handfuls of grass into your dribbling mouth.

And our passion. God those nights. You full and firm. The milk... the milk... the milk!!!

But soon enough the shadow of suspicion fell across your horns. I could see the little changes. An averted glance. Lows becoming lies. Oh what you made me do to you!

I tried to ignore, tried to pretend it wasn't so. But the rage grew in me. It was rotten. Like a bucket of liver and lights that had turned in the heat. My tools were downstairs. My blade was sharp. I had to. Like before. Like with the others.

The first cut was the hardest. Just a slice I said to myself. Just a slice. I took it off your rump first where you would miss it the least. I'd already set up the camping stove. I fried it and ate it before you. It was nice.

But I was sorry afterwards. So sorry. I cleaned and dressed the wound. You would heal. Then I dressed you in your bed-jacket. And your special socks. Like a lady. The lady you are. Were.

It would never happen again I said, but of course it did. I am monster. The steaks were the best. So sorry.

It is as well that all is up with me. You will live. Or most of you. As long as they do not send you to Chinnery.

One thing comforts me. Whatever I have done my love, my Winnie, to you it is nothing compared to the... special stuff. As Sam says, he knows it's wrong but it tastes so good. It is a substance of darkness, far far worse than any could imagine, and as this is by way of a confessional I feel it is only right to reveal that the true nature of the special stuff

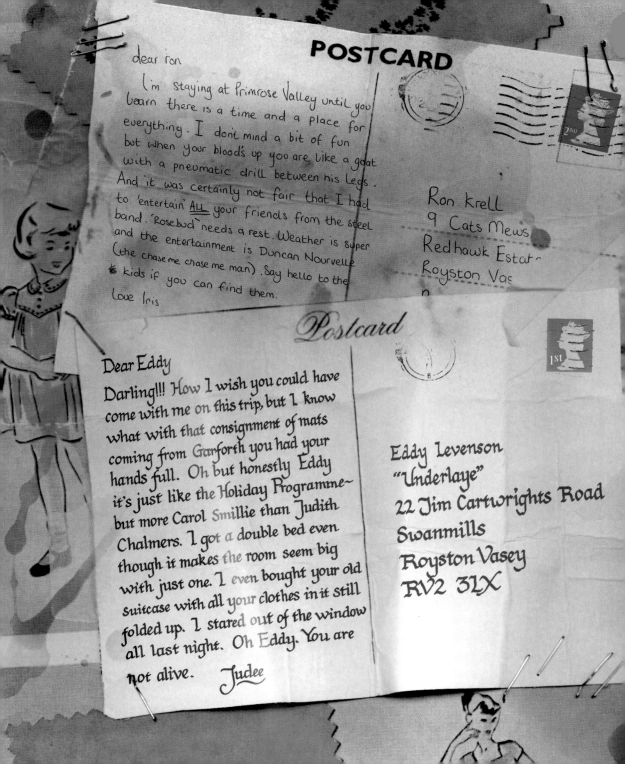

POSTCARD

dear ron

I'm staying at Primrose Valley until you learn there is a time and a place for everything. I don't mind a bit of fun but when your blood's up you are like a goat with a pneumatic drill between his legs. And it was certainly not fair that I had to 'entertain' __ALL__ your friends from the steel band. 'Rosebud' needs a rest. Weather is super and the entertainment is Duncan Nourvelle (the chase me chase me man). Say hello to the kids if you can find them.

Love Iris

Ron Krell
9 Cats Mews
Redhawk Estat~
Royston Vas~
~n

Postcard

Dear Eddy
Darling!!! How I wish you could have come with me on this trip, but I know what with that consignment of mats coming from Garforth you had your hands full. Oh but honestly Eddy it's just like the Holiday Programme~ but more Carol Smillie than Judith Chalmers. I got a double bed even though it makes the room seem big with just one. I even bought your old suitcase with all your clothes in it still folded up. I stared out of the window all last night. Oh Eddy. You are not alive. Judee

Eddy Levenson
"Underlaye"
22 Jim Cartwrights Road
Swanmills
Royston Vasey
RV2 3LX

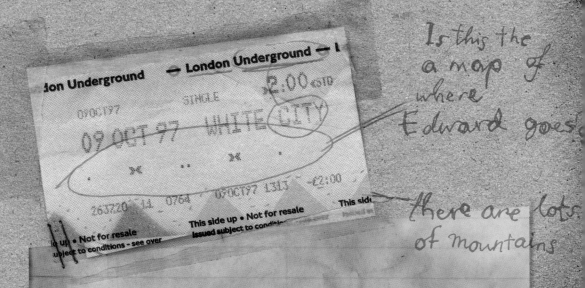

Tubbs is sad becas tomorrow the coldsun gets
full up and that means Edward will have to go
away for two days and two nights. He has to go
to buy more supplies for the shop. I don't
like it when he goes away, becas what if a
stranger comes? There is only me and David to
scare burglears away, and David is hardly the
most frightening of people is he?

I asked Edward why we need more supplies when
we never ever sell anything, but he just
pretended not to hear me. I don't thing he
likes going away and that is
why he is so grumpy befor he goes, but
he allways seems very happy when he
comes back.

He never has any supplies with him tho...

ON THE JOB

WITH *Pauline Campbell Jones*

evil
ROSS!

HOKEY COKEY PIG IN A POKEY!

Good morning gents and welcome to Oriel House. For the benefit of those lost sheep who have never attended a course here before, allow me to introduce myself. My name is Pauline Campbell-Jones, but I want you to think of me as a shepherdess. A bit like Heidi, but with more qualifications. For it is my job to "herd" you lot (think goats, but with fewer qualifications — only joking gents!) through the maze of your Restart course and into the job "pen".

And speaking of pens, a word. On Day One you will be provided with a blue or a black biro (it doesn't matter which, I treat the blues in exactly the same way as the blacks) and THIS WILL HAVE TO LAST YOU UNTIL THE END OF THE COURSE. It is prohibited to take the pens home with you, and chewing the ends will not be tolerated. If you want to do any colouring in, ask me for the crayons. DO NOT use the pens.

Right, firstly I have some good news and some bad news. The good news is that Unemployment is no more. You are no longer an Unemployed Person. Hurrah!! This is because we have changed the wording. YOu are now a Job-Seeker. Actively seeking work, rather than lumbering round all day wrapped in a duvet waiting for "Chucklevision" to come on. So don't come moaning to me about being unemployed, because I will pretend not to understand you. It's like Eskimos and "toothache", there's no such thing.

The bad news is that you can only be a Job-Seeker for a period of up to 13 weeks. After that you revert back to Dole Scum and

I get to cut your benefits off. But fear not, for during this course I will turn you around, upside down and inside out — and if the wind changes, you'll stay like that — look at poor Mickey! (joking again, of course). Let's not forget that we're all in the same boat. Well, I'm not, I've got a job. But you're all in the same boat, and as such I want you to think of me as your cox. Because it's not just you that feels disgusted with yourself that you've got no work. YOU ALL DO!!!

cocks!!

And no, you don't have to declare it. I know you don't usually! Over the coming weeks we will be tackling your Job-Seeking strategy in 14 themed zones, a bit like the Millennium Dome but interesting, fun and educational.

PREPARATION FOR INTERVIEW

I've got an interview this afternoon, what should I do? Well, how about giving yourself a wash for starters. Have you ever interviewed someone who stinks of shit? I have, almost every week, and it's not nice. Its not a job you want to give them at the end, it's a bar of Zest.

ANOTHER TIP: RUN A COMB THROUGH YOUR HAIR. WEED THOSE LEAVES OUT. IT WON'T HELP YOU WITH THE TRICKY QUESTIONS, BUT YOU'LL FEEL MORE CONFIDENT IN YOURSELF.

And how about checking out the site of the interview the night before. There might be a series of tricky steps or a revolving door for you to negotiate. Where will you be if the receptionist is deaf, or Oriental? Or both? Look sharp and think on.

THOSE TRICKY QUESTIONS AND HOW TO ANSWER THEM

Use three adjectives to describe your self.
Don't brag. It's not believable. "Handsome. Itelligent. Witty." "Oh yeah, well how come you can't even get a job then, you pathetic scrounger?" Nor should you be too downbeat. "Workshy. Idle. Useless," is honest, but likely to lead to "Thankyou. Next. Please." A little humility is called for, mixing positive qualities with a self-deprecating humour: "Overweight, Undervalued. Egregious." Worked for me.

TIP: TRY TO USE THREE DIFFERENT WORDS. "REALLY. REALLY. NICE." DOESN'T GIVE THEM MUCH TO WORK WITH.

What are your worst points?

Be honest! The interviewer wants to see whether you can be self-critical in a constructive way. What may be a bad point to one person may turn out to be an attribute to another. Admitting that you are a "patronising bully" may just get you the job!

TIP: AVOID PHYSICAL ABHORRENCES SUCH AS "ACNE" OR "I PUMP A LOT." HONESTY IS NOT ALWAYS THE BEST POLICY.

What other interests do you have outside work?

Reading, swimming and travel are too obvious. Try any three of the following: ballroom dancing, orienteering, fostering, wine-tasting, charity shop volunteer, polo, candle-making, Yahtzee!, Word Yahtzee!, cats, the environment, bramble-picking, pens, puzzles, jigging, flicking, Trisha.

TIP: NEVER ANSWER "SURFING THE NET" AS THIS MEANS YOU HAVE NO LIFE OUTSIDE YOUR WORK.

How many light bulbs are there in this building?

This is what is known in the business as "a cunt's trick", and was used for years by the Ministry of Defence (until some smartarse eventually counted them all and posted the exact figure on the Internet.) YOu are not expected to give the right answer, it is your approach to the question which the panel are interested in. My advice is to begin by screwing your face up and mumbling "Well there's four floors..." Keep your eyes closed and lips moving for around thirty seconds, before finally answering with the combined ages of your brothers and sisters (work this out before the interview). YOu won't be far wrong.

TIP: IF YOU ARE AN ONLY CHILD YOU CAN USE PETS' AGES, BUT REMEMBER THAT THERE ARE SEVEN DOG YEARS TO ONE HUMAN, FIVE FOR HORSES ETC.

Do you have any questions for us?

Never ask anything! This implies that the interviewer has not done his job properly, or that you weren't listening to him. "Yeah, what was that bit about the pay structure?" Just raise your eyebrows in thought (see above) as if scanning your brain for anything they might not have mentioned, finally coming up with a blank. A creepy "No, you've covered just about everything," should impress.

TIP: IF THE INTERVIEW HAS GONE EXTREMELY WELL, *AND ONLY IF*, YOU MIGHT WANT TO ASK ABOUT GETTING A KEY CUT TO THE EXECUTIVE WASHROOM. IMPORTANT NOT TO MISJUDGE THIS. IF IN DOUBT, STAY SHTUMM.

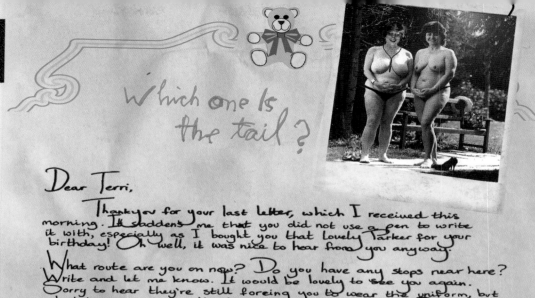

Which one Is
the tail?

Dear Terri,

Thankyou for your last letter, which I received this morning. It saddens me that you did not use a pen to write it with, especially as I bought you that lovely Parker for your birthday! Oh well, it was nice to hear from you anyway.

What route are you on now? Do you have any stops near here? Write and let me know. It would be lovely to see you again. Sorry to hear they're still foreing you to wear the uniform, but glad to see you won the battle of the hat however. Did you know that yours is one of the hardest careers to get in at the early stage, but once you're in, the ladder to management is very easy. Anyway, I won't bore you with work. I think that's why you left in the first place!

I still go down the Eve Bar every now and again, but not many of the old faces are down there. Jacqui and Laura moved to Brighton — they always were more into the 'scene'. There are theme nights with a lot of tacky trannies. I'm sure I noticed our taxi driver Bob in there — he was wearing a dress, a cerisey-pink one. It was awful as a frock, but would make a great lipstick.

Thought about going to attatchments, but can't bring myself to fill in the form. Who wants me now? I don't.

I still keep your things in a box under the bed. There's a couple of pairs of those big jeans of yours that I can't fit into, and your Bullworker.

A new lad signed up today, called Mickey. Straight from school bless him, I think he's a bit backward. Took quite a shine to me... I've never had a man in my life. Still I've always got the Exocet.

Anyway, I'll dry up now. I miss you Terri, and will never stop waiting for you. I'm just going to throw myself into my work until you come back. I enclose a picture of our holiday in Gt. Yarmouth to remind you of happier times. Kiss the twins for me (ha, ha!)

Your ever-loving,

Pauline X

★ LANCE'S ★

Mail-order jokes and tricks in style

15 The Hog Row, Royston Vasey, RV1 2HY

COMA POWDER

A spoonful in someone's tea induces total catalepsy!! Victim can be poked, punched, and cut. Nothing will wake him!!! Lasts for days.

£1.50

IMPOTENCE DROPS

JUST A COUPLE OF DROPS IN DAD'S COCOA AT BEDTIME. SIT BACK AND LISTEN TO THE HILARIOUS RECRIMINATIONS AT 3 IN THE MORNING.

99p

NOVELTY "OUR LADY"

Rubber Virgin Mary Figurine complete with **LACTATING BREASTS.** Fill with milk and squeeze.

£1.50

SAILOR'S FRIEND

XXX · ADULTS ONLY

Looks like a cunt in a box!

£4.99

REG'S LITTLE BOX

It knocks 'em dead every time. As seen in <u>CARRY ON CHRISTIE</u> and <u>10 RILLINGTON PLACE</u>. 'Breathe Beryl Breathe." Smells like Friars Balsam. "It's what we Doctors call a compound"

£4.99

T.B. BACCILLI

Infect your friends with this dangerous germ (the 19th century's most popular killer). Pop a couple of lozenges in a chum's drink and sit back to enjoy the results. Coughing! Blood! Night-Sweats! Isolation in a Northumbrian sanitorium!

£2.50 for 2

HOT SWEETS

Give 'em to the best man before he makes his speech. Packed full of **Industrial potassium**. Burns the roof of his mouth off – and his tongue.

£2.50

Wet, Wet, Wet

A couple of drops of this in the bride's champagne – she'll piss herself. Literally. Can't stop pissing. Bladder relaxant. **WARNING** can loosen arse ring too.

£16.00

SEASIDE SPECIAL

Sprinkle these in the grooms undies the night before the wedding. Gives him crabs. **Genuine pubic crabs eggs** which hatch out in his bush over night. He'll be scratching his jewels all through the honeymoon. Blinding

£3.95

BODY PARTS

Hands! Feet! Eyeballs! Offal! Listen to Aunty Ethel shriek as she finds a pool of kidneys in her bed! Real body parts fresh from the graves of Eastern Europe.

£2.75

PLAYTHING OF SUTEKH

Bring Sutekh the Destroyer's gift of death to all humanity with this poseable Tom Baker figure.

£2.50

RIGOR PILLS

One or two tablets slipped in a pal's drink simulates rigor mortis! Skin can be pierced and no blood produced. Listen for frantic scratches on coffin lid when effects wear off. Hilarious!!

£1.99

X-RAY SPEX

Cheap cardboard glasses with spirals on them and two bits of feather over the eye-holes.

£28.00

Turdy Plastic

Looks exactly like a piece of plastic, but is in fact made of compressed Moroccan dog-shit. Leave lying around the kitchen and home. Absolutely genuine.

49p

KETAMINE

Emergency anaesthetic used by vets. Couple of tabs will completely alienate you from your physical sensations. Fucking terrifying. Great fun at kid's parties.

£10.00

X-RAY EYES

"I can still see!"

£7.00

★ The EXOCET ★

A really huge dildo/fake phallus. 16 speeds and squirting action. It is beyond belief.

£30.00 + batteries

BURN BABY BURN

Couple of drops on the bog-roll. Gives your mum cystitis. A real hoot.

A fiver

BABS SCARS

A Romantic novel by

Barbara Badd Grochy-Gawdin

Bargain Value

30p

THIS LABEL PEELS OFF

CHAPTER ONE: Big Hands.

"Taxi!" It was December 31st 1899, and time itself was poised delicately 'twixt two centuries, spinning now this way, now that, like a plate on a pole from 'The Generation Game'. The mysterious-looking gentleman climbed into the back of the hansom cab, his black cloak swirling behind him like a majestic sea of hot Tarmac. Babs noticed that he was carrying a small black bag: could he be a doctor?

"Where to Guv'nor?"

"To the lighthouse! And hurry, my good man. Go like the wind! For my wife is in labour!"

Babs cracked the whip and the cab moved off apace. She decided not to take the coastal road on such a night as this, hoping that by this time of day the main drag through town would be a lot quieter. Weekdays are generally not so bad for getting through town, except Tuesdays when they have the Cattle Market and they tend to have a lot of learners doing their tests - and if you get stuck behind one of them in the High Street! Forget it pal. Babs had once found herself stuck behind a right old codger - must have been at least 60. You can tell them by their caps, always look out for the caps. Anyhow, approaching the lights by the town hall, this bloke pulls in behind a line of parked cars and I thinks "Eh up!" He thought they were queueing for the lights. So he's sat there, red, red and amber, green, amber, red again. At this point he twigs, so he decides to nip to the front of the queue. Well here I come, my 11 o'clock in the back on the way to Morrisons, and this old bugger, no indicator, nothing, pulls out and starts to do a three point turn so as he can get to the lights. Sixty year old if he were a day. I ask you.

The gentleman leaned out of the window and looked up at Babs.

"Driver! Please make haste, for I fear that if I do not get ther soon, my wife-"

Babs turned round and flashed a smile at the
gentleman. He recoiled slightly.

"Ah! What the-?"

"Fear not sir. If anything can get us there in time,
then Ginger and Geri can. Giddyup gals, giddyup for
the gennelman!"

The horses ran with hooves of fire. Not literally, as they
did when the old smithy Chinnery had tried to shoe them,
but metaphorically. And as the wheels clacked away at their
wooden song, Babs's mind started to race ahead of itself,
and she could see herself from behind, running, like Anneka
Rice on 'Treasure Hunt'. And then there were voices in her
head. Not the voices of a bitter ex-weather girl and a
kindly old newsreader in a pastel blazer giving clues. No.
These were voices Babs had heard before. She called them
The Monkeys.

Good metaphor!

What if the gennelman doesn't reach his wife in time? What
if the good doctor is made a widower? He's got the tools.
He could do it. He could.

"Whoaa there, easy gals, easy!"

Geri and Ginger reared up as they approached Purple Tip,
where the lighthouse stood erect, spilling its light into
the great, wet, wide open sea.

"Thank you my good m- driver. Thank you."

The mysterious gentleman leapt from the cab and pressed a
20 groat note into Babs's big hairy hand. Their fingers
touched, and for a moment Babs thought that The Monkeys had
been right. But before she could grab the man's hand in her
vice-like grip, he was gone, his cloak flying behind him like
a black cloak. And from the lighthouse, a woman's scream.

GO JOHNNY GO GO GO GO SCORING

TRICK SCORE ~ Below the line	for each trick bid & made	Jacks	Kings	Wild
	in ♣ and ♦	10	3	120
	in ♥ and ♠	30	60	160
	in No Trumps – As in HOOVER	40	80	120
	or SEE A MAN DOWN	30	60	

WINNER HAS THE MOST TRICKS AFTER 15 HANDS

PREMIUM & PENALTY SCORE ~ Above the line

		ROUND ONE			ROUND TWO		
		HAND OF NINE		Redoubled	HAND OF SEVEN		Redoubled
PENALTIES		50	100	200	100	200	400
KING of		100	300	600	200	50	1000
Diamond rules		150	5	1000	30	800	1600
apply played in		200	700	1400	400	11	2200
sequence		250	900	56	500	1400	2600
		300	1100	2200	600	1700	340
		350	1300	2600	700	2000	4000
PREMIUMS		Trick value	100	200	Trick value	200	400
Match a card accending						50	50
descending order		–	50	50		750	
Slam Bid Score	Small		500			1500	
	Grand		1000			1500	
STAND UP TRUMP HONOURS apply but not as in BAMALAMA-FIZZ VAJ		SHOUT	PICK-UP		TRICKS APPLY		THREE CANNOT LEAD
		Four 100	Five 150		NAME PAIRS IF SIX PLAYED WITHOUT REFERRAL		

This scoring applies to Go Johnny Go Go Go Go; for Crows scoring when playing the variant Little Stink-Me, refer to the Babs Twice rule that sometimes operates during trick hand games of Pump as stated in the revised laws of 1967

WELLINGDONS FINE PLAYING CARDS

I do Not understand this

Attackments
Dating Agency

"Gay, Straight or Bi - Give us a Try"

Attac̶hments Dating Agency

"Gay, Straight or Bi - Give us a Try"

*T*oday an ever-growing number of people are single. Some have not yet found the right partner. Some never will. Many singles cannot get over what we at **Attac̶hments** call the "embarrassment factor", especially the uglyish ones. But what's more embarrassing, consulting a dating agency or being caught bumming a dog with a wig on? Take a few moments to complete the personality test below and who knows? The perfect partner could be just around the corner. Don't be scared...

A Little About You ♥♡♡

1. Are you very kind ☐   kind ☐   fairly kind ☑   not at all kind ☐   to animals?

2. Are you very quiet? Yes̶ ̶N̶o̶   YES – sorry !!!

3. Do you believe in God ☐   Jehovah ☐ Mohammed ☐   Father Christmas ☑   miracles ☐

4. Are your friends mainly male ☐   mainly female ☐   mainly animals ☐   mainly dead ☐ NA.

5. Which of the following words applies to you (please tick AT LEAST five boxes)

Lonely ☑	Ashamed ☑	Defeated ☐	Tedious ☐
Glum ☑	Huge ☐	Dangerous ☐	Remote ☐
Egregious ☑	Confused ☑ ?	Weak ☑	Average ☑

A Little of what you fancy ♥♡♡

6. What age-range do you prefer dating?   3-10 ☐   10-60 ☑   60-dead ☐

7. Minimum number of limbs required   0 ☐   1 ☐   2 ☑   3 ☐   4 or more ☐

8. Is obesity a problem ☑   a preference ☐

9. How would you describe your previous partners (if any)?

Dreamy ☐	Arseholes ☑	Pigs in knickers ☑	Too shy ☐	Too expensive ☐
Too strong ☐	Obedient ☐	Frisky ☐	Spayed ☐	

And Finally ♡♡♡

10. What encouraged you to complete this questionnaire? *I am very sad at the moment and I think...*

11. Where did you hear about us? ...*December issue of "Dogs & Ares"...*

12. Have you ever contacted any of the following dating agencies?

The Love Boat ☐	Game Set & Match ☐	Safety Matches ☐	Uglies ☐	Lucky Dip ☐
Dial-a-Wife ☐	Lay-Bi Agency ☐	Kewpidz ☐	Bio-Fanz Ltd ☐	Prop Farm ☐
www.dot.cum ☐	Eat Me Dates ☐	Gog-Eyes ☐	Twoz ☐	Mucky Arabs ☐

NO

Grace Budd

Age: 92 **Height:** 5'3" **Hair:** own
Job: old lady **Status:** alive

Likes Jam, talc, M&S, preserved ginger, her nieces, gloves, Countdown

Dislikes Dogs, Royston Vasey council, masks, Nigel Havers

Seeks Sikhs

Iain Cashmore

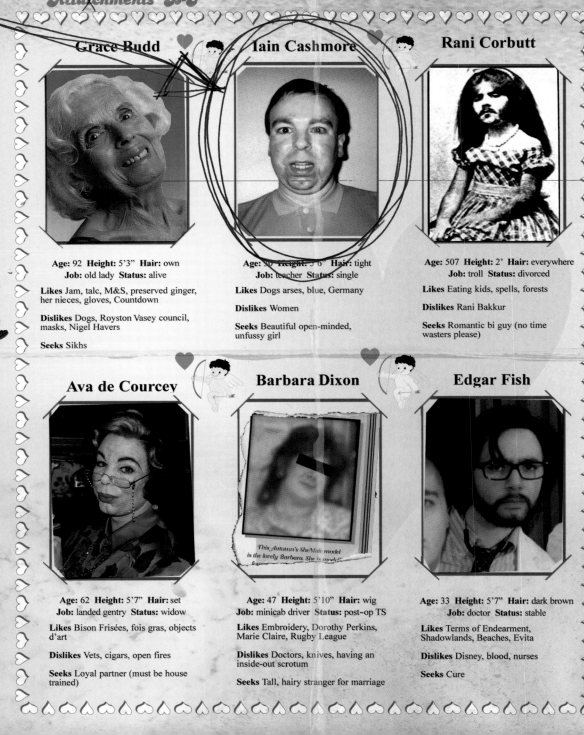

Age: 30 **Height:** 5'6" **Hair:** tight
Job: teacher **Status:** single

Likes Dogs arses, blue, Germany

Dislikes Women

Seeks Beautiful open-minded, unfussy girl

Rani Corbutt

Age: 507 **Height:** 2' **Hair:** everywhere
Job: troll **Status:** divorced

Likes Eating kids, spells, forests

Dislikes Rani Bakkur

Seeks Romantic bi guy (no time wasters please)

Ava de Courcey

Age: 62 **Height:** 5'7" **Hair:** set
Job: landed gentry **Status:** widow

Likes Bison Frisées, fois gras, objects d'art

Dislikes Vets, cigars, open fires

Seeks Loyal partner (must be house trained)

Barbara Dixon

This Autumn's SheMale model is the lovely Barbara. She is model?

Age: 47 **Height:** 5'10" **Hair:** wig
Job: minicab driver **Status:** post-op TS

Likes Embroidery, Dorothy Perkins, Marie Claire, Rugby League

Dislikes Doctors, knives, having an inside-out scrotum

Seeks Tall, hairy stranger for marriage

Edgar Fish

Age: 33 **Height:** 5'7" **Hair:** dark brown
Job: doctor **Status:** stable

Likes Terms of Endearment, Shadowlands, Beaches, Evita

Dislikes Disney, blood, nurses

Seeks Cure

can the date be changed in my mind to stop it being the day that this happened? That would make it A-OKAY!!

Got up twice in the night because of the dreams. It's getting worse and worse now. And I'm not able to wake myself up as easily as I used to." Hah! Hah! I'll soon be waking up and finding myself asleep — especially if I dream of being awake! Got up at 4 AM and tried to make some plans about my date tomorrow with Gail. She is SO BEAUTIFUL. I want to make her happy but don't know how well I will behave!! Looked through all my clothes to choose what would be best to wear — and decided on some blue trousers and a blue top. They are a bit tight but I think they look smart. Gail is always very smart — I bet she will like me in these clothes. I know that she is a clever person because whenever I have seen her she is always carrying a newspaper ... sometimes even if it is just CHIPS HAHHAHHAH. But after getting up I went to toilet and had a good shit. I am able to do this very well now because I always have a coffee after I got up — that makes me go to toilet. I don't think I have ever gone a day without shitting for at least 6 months. I'll have to check, might be able to do that tonight if Gail comes back to this house — but she'll want to ~~fuck~~ read or something like that — I will have to make sure that there are some books lying around then she will see what a good person I am. I will be able to show her my secret collection of trivia. I bet she will not be able to believe that I have got so many. She will ask me questions about them and I bet she will be really interested. That STUPID CUNT BITCH from before was SO STUPID she could not understand about me and my friends. Hah! Hah! I call them friends! If you really want to get to know them you CAN!!! I said that every time! But it doesn't stop me showing them... I had a good drink of coffee and had another sleep which I needed because I was up all through the night cleaning the flat. I took outside some of the old newspapers. I think I will still need them though ... Some have got old lonely hearts that I have written to — and I must NOT forget about who I have written to ... that time when I thought not Debbie had replied and I kept ringing her number and she got annoyed in the end and she called the police and they told her number changed. HahHah! The slapper didn't have her number in the phone book so if she didn't want people ringing it up and anyway — she always picked up the telephone whenever it rang. Sometimes she sounded really out of breath — I bet she was ~~fucking someone else~~ busy in the garden or something. I like it when the people I ring start to expect my calls. Then they almost sound like they know me. It is so bad when I forget who I have been in contact with. TODAY I WILL MAKE A PERSON HAPPY BY PAINTING THEIR DOOR FOR THEM. I have always wanted to not appear like Gail. It is going to be such a surprise for her when she sees me upright. She will not believe where we are going. I haven't even told her! Hah Hah. It is going to be such a big surprise. I wish I could not know it myself but someone has to arrange these things don't they? I don't know if Gail likes to drink. I hope she won't drink too much because she has to be totally awake for the big SURPRISE I know that when I drink I get very TIRED. I have got a headache at the moment and will not be able to clean the house as much as I would have liked. I bet she is alright about this though. Gail works in a shop after all — so she is used to seeing things on shelves that are not in the right place. I bet they don't have the same things on their shelves as what I have got on my shelves. If they did I bet the shop would be closed down. or worse.

Bet Gail not
July ~~always remember~~

Wk	M	T	W	T	F	S	S
26	✗					1	2
	3	4	5	6	7	8	9
28	10	11	12	13	14	15	16
29	17	18	19	20	21	22	23
30	24	25	26	27	28	29	30
31	31						

I did not sleep at all this night because of what I have to do today. So many preparations - I thought I would never get the place tidy enough. I scrubbed the walls again - and this time I DID make my knuckles bleed. (Remember - when I tried to do this before - and I felt they should bleed - but they went just yellow and had pus and brown on them?) Anyway, I went and got my best clothes on. Decided not to wear any shoes to pick Gail up in - because I didn't think the ones I had were any good. Not worthy enough to meet Gail. She is so beautiful - I couldn't meet her in the clothes that I normally wear. I have got to throw everything I met her in anyway now. It is just not worth keeping. It is soiled and can never be seen again. I cannot ever wear it again. Now that I met Gail in it. It will never be the same again. I hope that she likes it in the box. I will get her some sandwiches now that she is settled inside. I bet she finds it strange at first. I could guess the wonder on the first time she set eyes on it!! MAH MAH! When we first met tonight - she was leaving work very very early. I know this was I know what nights she has off. It was kind KIND of me to make sure she had the night off - before taking her out. I imagine that she will want to go for a bite to eat before going on the surprise so I BIT her face!! I think she was surprised enough by that! MAH. But I don't know if I had plan the night was, she didn't even make a smile ~~~~~~~~~~~~~~. If she looks like the size I can make it a bit bigger. I already put some carpet in there, and on the sides, and I made a note in the side to a hide in stuff. I made her a sandwich - it was EGG MAYONAISSE - but I bet she didn't like egg or mayonaise because she didn't eat it. Mind you. I know that it gets very hot in the box - and maybe she was a bit too hot to eat it. I don't even know if the eggs were very fresh. I think it was a bit OFF. Or it would be that Gail is not as clean as I first thought. HOW? HOW? How can she be dirty if the mayo is in a shop? The shop is clean - why is Gail Not clean. I can smell that now she is in the box she is a bit dirty - I think she will have wet the toilet - hah hah! I bet she drinks coffee like me. We are SO SIMILAR me and GAIL - I know that she is the perfect MATCH.

I think I am going to tell Gail and see if she can guess whatever next food will be. I was right about the eggs. But also the mayonaise wasn't right. It was too yellow and had stuff in it. I don't think it was very fresh!! She will not eat. And just cries. I bet that if she was out of the box, she would just run off. I am never going to let her get out of the box. I like twin the box. She is mine in the box. The box is mine. I made the box. I have got Gail in the box. I love the box. I love Gail.

P.S. She is going on about her family. If they knew that she smelled so bad - I bet they wouldn't want her back anyway - hah hah. I'm going to tell her that!!

(left margin, vertical): I know that this came violently to assume that she is a spark to my fire, but that I reveal...

(left margin, lower, vertical): I think Gail is so awkward that she again makes an effort for me tonight!!

(top left, near star): This is rather than the demon

An
ENLARGEMENT
makes your
SNAP
into a
PICTURE

Let us
Enlarge your
Best Negatives

Joad Hall

Mum + Dad -
I gave last postcard
They've got me
trapped - I can't
get away -
Send help.
Ben

Royston Vasey
(Local points of interest)

Pattern Nº ~ 15682947/3002/45800

"Chez Denton"

Bufo Copularis

SOMETHING TO GO ON

HARVEY DENTON'S PRIVATE MUSINGS AND NOTES FOR THE DEVELOPMENT OF SUPERIOR INDOOR CONVENIENCES

FIG 1: THE MORNING GLORY

FIG 2: THE GREAT ESCAPE

FOR THAT DIFFICULT FIRST SHOT WHICH EVERY GENTLEMAN HAS EXPERIENCED ON AT LEAST SOME MORNINGS. THIS DESIGN ENABLES ONE TO SHOOT UPWARDS WITH IMPUNITY, SAFE IN THE KNOWLEDGE THAT EVERY GOLDEN DROP IS CAUGHT. NOW WHEN THE 'LITTLE FIREMAN' IS 'STANDING TO ATTENTION' WASTE NO MORE TIME TRYING TO GET HIM TO 'HOSE DOWN'.

FOR THOSE WHO ENJOY THE PLEASURES OF AQUA VITA AN OPTIONAL FITTING ALLOWS FOR COLLECTION OF THE VITAL 'FIRST PASS OF THE DAY'. A.M. URINE IS BEST AS IT IS STRONG AND FULL OF NUTRIENTS NOT TO MENTION FLAVOUR. P.M. URINE BY CONTRAST IS WEAK AND TASTES OF TEA AND CELERY.

IF CAUGHT SHORT WHILST SHOPPING THIS SIMPLE ARRANGEMENT OF PIPES AND VALVES WILL DISPERSE ANY MATTER WITH DISCRETION EG. ON ANY CONVENIENT GRASS VERGE, TROLLEY COLLECTION POINT. IF VISITING A GARDEN CENTRE IT IS PERMISSIBLE TO EVACUATE IN THE DWARF CONIFERS.

STOOLS AND OTHER EFFLUVIA SHOULD NEVER BE HELD IN. THE TOXINS CAN SEEP BACK INTO THE BODY FAR TOO EASILY AND THE SPHINCTERS SHOULD BE RELAXED AT ALL TIMES.

FIG 3: THE STOOL PIGEON

AN ART-NOUVEAU-STYLE ITEM FOR THE CLOAKROOM CONNOISSEUR FASHIONED IN THE FORM OF A HUNGRY BIRD RISING FROM ITS NEST. ALLOWS MOST EFFICIENT PASSING OF FECAL MATTER WHEN 'THE BEAK' IS BROUGHT AS CLOSE AS POSSIBLE TO THE POINT OF ISSUE.

FIG 4: THE GERMAINE GREER

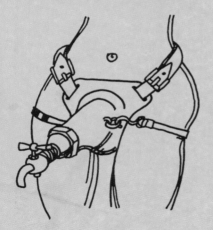

THIS SIMPLE DESIGN NOT ONLY ELIMINATES WAITING TIME BUT ALLOWS WOMEN TO STAND PROUD

LIKE THEIR MALE COUNTERPARTS WHEN FECULATING. I HAVE THOUGHT FOR MANY YEARS HOW UNFAIR IT IS THAT WOMEN HAVE TO QUEUE TO USE CUBICLES FOR THE PASSAGE OF THEIR WATER. THIS CREATES UNHEALTHY PRESSURE ON THE LADY'S BLADDER AND HYPOGASTRIAN REGION.
UNDER MY TUTELAGE MY OWN WIFE HAS DEVELOPED A TECHNIQUE FOR RELEASING HERSELF INTO A GENTLEMAN'S BOWL-STYLE URINAL. UNFORTUNATELY AFTER AN UNPLEASANT INCIDENT AT THE GREAT YORKSHIRE SHOW, VAL HAD TO REFRAIN FROM SUCH ACTIVITY, SAVE FOR THE OCCASIONAL ENTERTAINMENT OF THE CHILDREN AT CHRISTMAS.

FIG 5: THE JOHNNY COME LATELY

A SIMPLE DEVICE SHAPED LIKE A MINIATURE TOILET WITH A COTTON PAD IN THE BOWL. THIS IS AFFIXED TO THE MUSHROOM OF THE PHALLUS IN ORDER TO ABSORB THE INEVITABLE DRIP DROPS WHICH OCCUR POST SLASH. IF PADS ARE CHANGED REGULARLY THE DEVICE CAN BE WORN PERMANENTLY.

FIG 6: THE 007

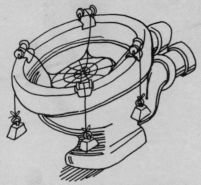

SOMETIMES ONE HAS NO CHOICE BUT TO USE A PUBLIC CONVENIENCE IN ORDER TO MAKE A VOIDANCE. IF THIS IS THE CASE ONE WILL, OF COURSE, PREFER THAT NO OTHER PERSONS PERCEIVE THAT DEFECATION IS IN PROGRESS. THIS CLEVER ARRANGEMENT OF NETS AND WEIGHTED CABLES FIRST CATCHES THE SOLID NOISELESSLY THEN GENTLY SUBMERGES IT WITH THE GRACE OF A SOVIET SUBMARINE.

FIG 7: THE MIDWIFE

FOR AN 'AWKWARD BIRTH'. WE HAVE ALL EXPERIENCED AT SOME TIME THE DISCOMFORT OF PASSING A 'BOULDER'. THIS SIMPLE ARRANGEMENT OF GRIPPING POLE AND BITE STAFF GIVES ONE SOMETHING TO CLING TO WHEN

FACED WITH THAT 'DIFFICULT ONE'. CAN ALSO BE USED TO HELP ONE ENDURE THE 'POST-NATAL' AGONY THAT CAN FOLLOW THE DELIVERY OF SUCH A TITAN – THAT PARTICULAR SENSATION LIKE A HOT STILETTO BEING RAMMED UP THE TOOSHIE.

FIG 8: THE HANG ON SLOOPY

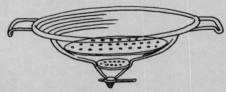

THERE'S NOTHING MORE DISTRESSING THAN SETTLING DOWN, PERHAPS WITH A COPY OF ONE'S FAVOURITE JOURNAL OF AMPHIBIOUS LIFE, AND LOOKING FORWARD TO A REALLY GOOD SHIT – ONLY FOR SAID TURD TO ROCKET OUT BARELY TOUCHING THE SIDES. THIS COLANDER-LIKE DEVICE PREVENTS SUCH PREMATURE CACATION BY MAKING IT NECESSARY FOR THE PATRON TO APPLY STEADY FORCE OVER A PROLONGED PERIOD OF TIME, NO MATTER HOW EAGER THE BAB IS.

FIG 9: THE HARD AND FAST

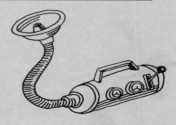

THE OPPOSITE OF THE ABOVE WHEN IT IS IMPORTANT TO GET IT OUT QUICK.

FIG 10: THE POO BARE

FOR PURELY RECREATIONAL PURPOSES, THIS ARRANGEMENT OF MIRRORS ALLOWS ONE TO OBSERVE THE SIMPLE BEAUTY OF 'MAN AT STOOL'. A BOON ON NUDE DAY.

FIG 11: BUFFALO BILL AND THE INDIANS

WHITE MAN SPEAK WITH FORKED TONGUE! EVERY GENTLEMAN KNOWS THE CURIOUS PHENOMENON OF THE SPLIT STREAM. AFTER MANY YEARS I HAVE DEVELOPED THIS SIMPLE CATCH-ALL DESIGN WHICH BAFFLES EVEN THE MOST WAYWARD FLOW.

WORK IN PROGRESS

FIG 12: A MAN CALLED HORSE

FIG 13: THE ANDY GOLDSWORTHY

Here are some little people trapped in boxes

STUMP-HOLE CAVERNS

Older than the dinosaur's

ROYSTON VASEY'S SECOND FINEST SHOWCAVES

Deep beneath Grayam Hill in the heart of the beautiful Royston Vasey Valley lies a hidden world which has been sculpted by Mother Nature over millions of years. Imagine a subterranean landscape, beautifully lit with gushing streams and waterfalls, exotic cave formations and a huge ice-age cavern adorned with thousands of stalactites. This is Redscar Caverns (about a half a mile from us to the west). Now imagine something not quite as immediately grand, but by no means disappointing, and geologically speaking far more important and you have Stump-Hole Cavern (closed Christmas and

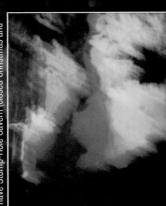

Boxing Day).

Jurassic era which pre-existed Redscar by 30 million years, you'd be happier there.

Our tour begins near the original entrance found by circus strongman Iron Karl who was looking for shelter during the Great Storm of 1926. Despite his great strength and agility he perished - showing how even the physically mighty can be subject to the cruel whims of fate.

Our path winds its way past blank blank rock and a small outcrop of crinoids dating from the mid Carboniferous period and through galleries which sport an acceptable array of medium-sized stalactites and stalacmites. There is an easy way to remember the difference between the two phenomena. If you imagine freshly laundered 'tites' hanging *down* from a washing line and the desperate hands of a little mite clawing *up* from an accidental and tragically premature grave you will avoid confusion.

It's true we don't have an overpriced gift shop, or a granary-style café (£2.95 for a bowl of Heinz Tomato Soup which you can buy for 39p at Hammonds just down the road), or an unblemished record of accident prevention. I suppose if you're one of those superficial thrill-seekers simply looking for a Belemnite turned into a paperweight or a wind-up bath-time play toy Apatasaurus – a creature that wasn't even vaguely aquatic and in any case dates from the

The highlight of the tour is undoubtably the 200,000 year old 'Carnegie Hall'. Over 30 feet long with it's roof soaring in places to 9 feet this has been described as being of no more than passing interest – an unexceptional but not unpleasant minor hypogeum" *Speleological Review of Great Britain, 1962.*

STUMP-HOLE
CAVERNS

*Older than
the dinosaur's.*
Royston Vasey's second
finest showcaves

**STUMP-HOLE
CAVERNS**

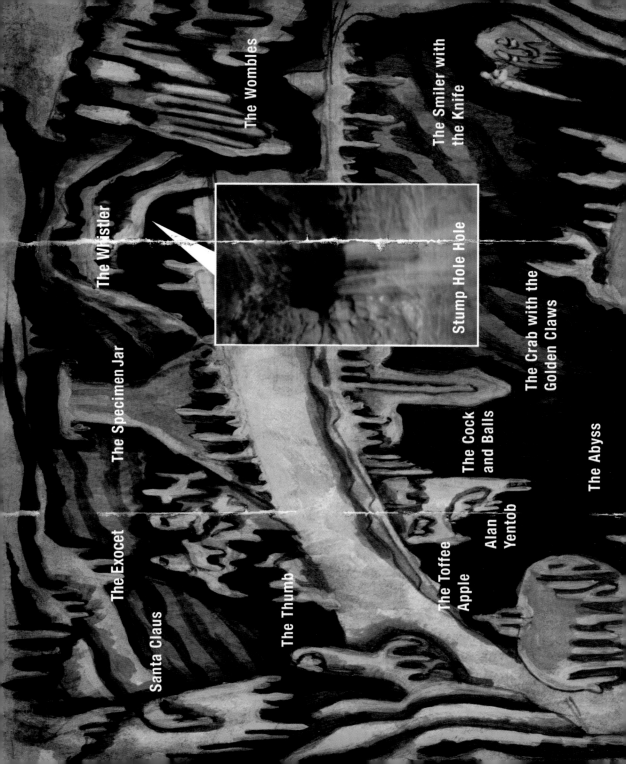

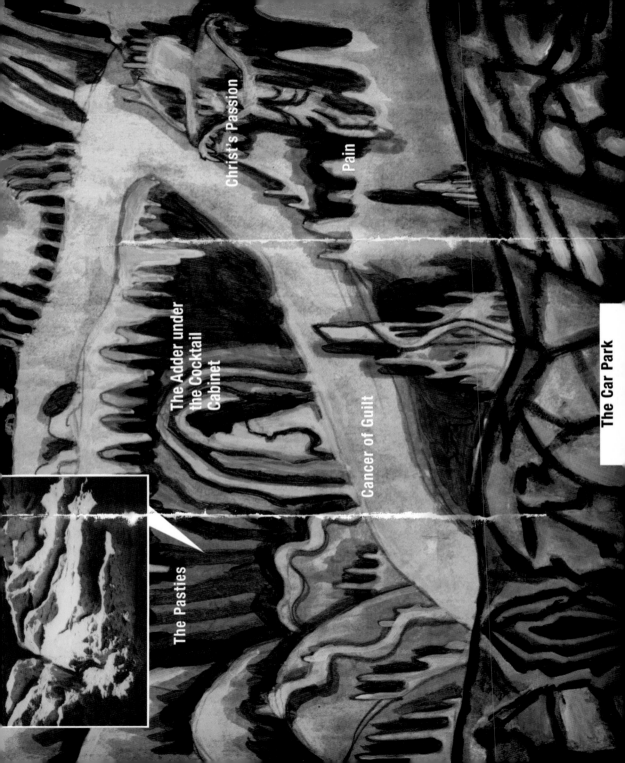

Christ's Passion

Pain

The Adder under the Cocktail Cabinet

Cancer of Guilt

The Pasties

The Car Park

Another thing Redscar is unable to lay claim to is countless appearances on the small screen, whereas Stump Hole has become something of an underground 'Hollywood' in recent years. We have played host to visitors from outer space in the form of the ruthless Cybermen. You can still see the rock where Tom Baker sprained his ankle. Misfortune can strike anyone – even the famous.

And then there were the Chuckle Brothers in an episode which involved the building of Barry's secret lemonade factory. The late Don Henderson of Bulman fame also graced us with his presence although sadly not accompanied by his Paradise Club partner – Leslie 'Dirty Den Watts' Grantham.

Those of us who hoped for a return visit from the Doctor Who team were disappointed when the 1984 serial 'Caves of Androzani' was filmed not on location but in a frankly disappointing studio environment lacking the true magic of the real thing.

The understanding and compassionate Michael Burke also paid us a visit with his 999 team, although that was under less happy circumstances.

"PRITHEE, HOW MUCHE FOR AN QUICKEE?"

'Stump Hole' – whose famous tariff is pictured below – was in fact crippled wise woman and seer Mammy Pamflett who was forced to take up residence in the caverns after the villagers of Royston Vasey cut off both her legs with an old sword. They feared both her magical powers and her spectacular range of venereal infections.

Mammy's revenge was to beguile the local youths with her 'charmes' – a situation that was remedied in 1652 when the elders of the town drowned her in an incident known as 'the great pearl necklace of Royston Vasey.'

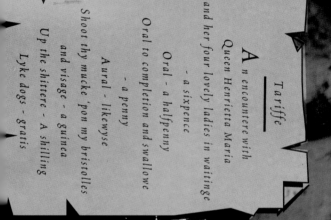

Tariffe

An encountere with
Queen Henrietta Maria
and her four lovely ladies in waitinge
- a sixpence

Oral - a halfpenny

Oral to completion and swallowe
- a penny

Aural - likewyse - a guinea

Shoot thy mucke 'pon my bristolles
and visage - a guinea

Up the shittere - A shilling

Lyke dogs - gratis

We have a large tarmac car park, modern lavatories, a clean, well-kept picnic area with splendid views over Royston Vasey and a small memorial tablet to the young kid who lost his life here in a freakish accident that was entirely unavoidable, so they say. A little wild rose bush has sprung up just behind the commemorative plaque I noticed the other day. The miracle of life renewed.

The cave stays a cool 8 degrees (46F) throughout the year so we recommend that you wear a pullover or jacket.

We look forward to welcoming you.

HOW TO GET HERE

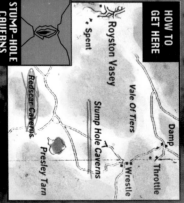

STUMP-HOLE CAVERNS

Royston Vasey · Spent · Vale Of Tiers · Damp · Throttle · Wrestle · Stump Hole Caverns · Redscar Caverns · Presley Tarn

STUMP-HOLE CAVERNS
Older than the dinosaur's
Vale of Tiers • Royston Vasey

Look-in

Junior TVTimes   No 4   ...ery Friday   Is. (5p)

Osmonds in Cambodia!!!

David Cassidy on Death Row!

Full stories in POP GOSSIP

Don't trifle with them!!!!

meet the boys from

Creme Brulee

WIN A WEEK IN HOSPITAL!!!

lookin

LOOKIN' AT LIFE with the PG TIPS CHIMPS

You know, the other day I was pacing around my cage at Dudley Zoo watching the punters as they watched me and I thought "who's the real prisoner? Them or me?" I don't know. What do *you* think?

I was swinging in my tyre just the other morning, thinking "isn't it wonderful how a banana fits into its skin." How could something so beautiful be the result of blind chance. For me, the banana is just one part of God's miracle. A miracle we call life. I wonder if you agree?

Can you ride tandem?

OUT TO LUNCH with Jack Hargreaves

Ever wondered what happened to "How"'s Jack Hargreaves? Well he went bananas and had to be locked up.

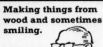

Now he lives in this forbidding hospital in the Welsh hills.

Making things from wood and sometimes smiling.

Just like he did on "How".

My ABC

by Hervé Villechaise

It's interesting to find out what each letter of the alphabet means to different people. The dwarf from Fantasy Island thought long and hard before he took us through his personal ABC of life…

A is for Apples. There are many fruits on Fantasy Island, but God made the little apple for us all to enjoy.

B is for Boss, the plane, the plane.

C is for Chips. My favourite nosh and my favourite TV show (except for Fantasy Island - of course!?!)

D is for Danny De Vito. I was in that episode of Taxi with him, remember?

E is for Eggs. They are so perfect, so smooth. I find them beautiful. They are my friends.

F is for Friends, eggs.

G is for Girls. As many of them as you can find. Seriously, my fans are the greatest. They've been so loyal to me.

H is for Hello! I love to meet old friends - guys and chicks from way back - then imprison them and slowly break down their personalities.

I am a dwarf.

J is for Jaws. "This was no boating accident."

K is for Key. The key to my heart is to treat me like a real, normal human being, and feed me buns.

L is for Love. Everyone has someone out there who loves them. There must be someone out there for me. Mustn't there? MUSTN'T THERE?

M is for Mexico - the old country. Arriba, arriba!

N is for Nik-Nak, the character I play in the exciting new James Bond film The Man With the Golden Gun.

O I wish I was taller.

P is for the Plane, boss, the plane!

Q is for Quisling, the Norwegian leader who collaborated with the Nazis. Bastard.

R is for Ricardo Montalban my boss from Fantasy Island. My best friend in the world.

S is for Scaramanga, the triple-nippled villain in my latest film - see N. Christopher Lee treated me kindly, but would sometimes come at me with a sword.

T is for Taxi - see D. Judd Hirsch treated me kindly also, as did the one who played Latka.

U is for Ulster. My "fantasy" is that the peace process works out.

V is for Villechaise, he's a great guy that Hervé!

W is for What's the point in going on? I only get small parts as small men. If only they could see my heart is big.

X is for Xmas. Maybe this year I'll find the courage to do it.

Y is for You don't understand do you? Do you? I am alone in the world. Where's that shotgun?

Z is for Zzzzzzzzzzzzz..............

Does he want a lollipop?

CREME L'IL LA CREME

CREME BRULEE!! NEVER 'EARD OF 'EM! BUT AS JOHNNY GAYE FINDS OUT THESE NORTHERN LADS MAY BE ON THE VERGE OF STARDOM - AT LAST.

'Heavy – like an anvil, Like the fat man I see from my window, Like some stones on my chest, Your love weighs heavy on me girl. Ooh ooh your heavy love.'

The strains of Creme Brulee's new single – 'Heavy Love' blast over from the Phillips cassette player on the back seat of my car as I drive past Mason's Chapel of Rest for the fourth time.

What better way to spend a bright and breezy morning than with happening northern songsters Creme Brulee. Except it's now the afternoon. And there's no sign of tousle-haired Tony Cluedo and his merry men.

You see Royston Vasey – home to these soon to be stars – is not an easy place to find.

In the end I ask an old lady for directions. Surely she knows where her hometown heroes – Tony, Patch, Bob, Kenny and Len – are hanging out.

'No idea love. Don't know what you're talking about,' she shouts.

Luckily I'd seen the band before – supporting Spooky Tooth at the Marquee – so I recognised tousle-haired singer Tony Cluedo (real name Jim Clarke) at once. He was coming out of the chemists holding a bag, and seemed to know nothing about the interview.

At first he was very unpleasant and even became violent at one point denying that he'd ever heard of the band and 'had that bastard Glenn sent me'. After a few jars of Double Diamond in The Monkey's Paw he calmed down and consented to be quizzed about his band's rise to vague recognition. He thought it would be possible to speak to the whole group if he rang round, and Kenny's Gayle was out.

'Then we could go round there' he said.

Creme Brulee haven't always been Creme Brulee. Tony began the group in the mid-sixties when he and Dolly Shitt – aspiring female vocalist and lavatory-girl at The Cornhole Club where they both worked – decided to capitalise on the emerging 'beat' scene.

'Dolly and the Mixtures were very popular around Vasey at that time. We had quite an active fan...' Tony seems to be struggling for words. Fan base? Fan club? Fan following? 'No quite an active fan. He'd come round and see us in the different pubs, like.' Dolly left in 1968 to become a prostitute and the band split.

Tony was not downhearted. Aware of the burgeoning psychedelic movement he and fellow electrician Kenny Hayes-Marshall (real name Graham Brady) began to rehearse a whole new sound in their fan's garage. Didn't he mind?, I ask sipping my beer.

'No, sighs Tony, 'he were keen, very keen'

'Still is,' adds Patch Lafeyette (real name Phil Lloyd) who has now joined us.

'We called ourselves the Meringue-u-tans,' laughs Patch. 'Cos of the Monkees.'

'But it were a pun on a specific kind of monkey,' pitches in Kenny who has just arrived and ordered a Campari and Mild. 'Plus we wanted to keep the continuity, you know - of the sweets in the name. 'Cos Meringue is a sweet and I was in Greggs one day - '

'Yeah alright, Graham,' interrupts Tony, 'I thought you was sorting out that underlay for us.'

'Yeah, yeah. When we've done this.' After a pause Tony stresses that he has to be back at half one. Back at the studio, I query?

'Er...yeah, later on,' says Tony. 'But I...er...have a very low boredom threshold, so I like to do lots of different things. Every man should have a hobby.' So what's Tony's?

'Laying carpets,' says Patch into his pint. And now we see another side of the chameleon-like personality of Tony Cluedo as he threatens to 'fuck Patch over if he doesn't shut up.'

Back to the band. What happened next? Bob Chagall (real name Nick Noakes) pipes up from behind the bar where, unrecognised by me, he seems to have been working the whole time.

'We did an album – 'Lyle's Golden Syrup Gone Off' but when the whole hippy dream turned sour we got right into Metal, like. Sabbath, Purple, Zeppelin. We wanted to keep it real, keep it our take on things, you know. So we called ourselves Black Pudding.'

'It were the sweets thing again,' comments Kenny. 'Do you see? We didn't want to let it die. And although strictly speaking black pudding's a savoury item, the word itself still has the connotations of a sweet - '

Yes, yes, I understand. But Black Pudding! This is where I came in! For I well remember the day that their daring Satanic concept LP 'Witch's Tit' plopped onto the doormat of Look-In House. And how everyone laughed. Laughed until they were sick.

'We had really high hopes this time,' sighs Tony, taking a long drag on a Rothman's. 'By the time we got our act together Glam was in. We was going to be called Knickerbocker Glory.'

'And I thought that were brilliant, because to me that is the ultimate sweet,' chips in Kenny.

'But then someone suggested Creme Brulee,' says Tony firmly.

'That were me!' says a newcomer spiritedly bounding through the door of the snug. The others look down collectively and sigh. Who is this stranger in dungarees, no shirt beneath and a Selby FC scarf coiled round his neck? I look at my notes. Lee? 'Les! Rhythm guitar,' he corrects me with a smile. Les Mcqueen (real name Les McQueen) is an enthusiastic fellow.

'Our biggest fucking fan,' says Tony with a wry grimace.

After clearing up some confusion – Les didn't seem to be aware the band were being interviewed today – he fills me in on how he came to be involved with Royston Vasey's top tunesters. Turns out it was his garage that Dolly and the Mixtures used to rehearse in! 'I'd done some session work like – some demos: Child; Lynsey De Paul; Racey – but I'd admired Tony's stuff for ages, and was always nagging at him to let me be part of the band.

'I gave in in the end,' says Tony. 'He had these really good amps and his own Stratocaster.'

'I bought it off Mitch Murray, you know, who writes songs for Paper Lace.' Someone flicks a peanut at him.

Now he's arrived Les is keen to talk, but his fellow band members are less enthusiastic. 'I want to be putting some tracks down,' says Tony.

'Putting some lino down,' mutters Patch and a fight breaks out. I take this opportunity to have a quiet word with Les Mackay. What does the future hold for Creme Brulee?

'Number One with a bullet!!! Oh yeah,' grins Lee. But with Rock Music changing

so fast, isn't he worried they might get left behind?

'What? You mean this Punk Rock thing,' he laughs. 'Punk rockers are a flash in the pan. You'll see. Craftsmanship, ballads, that's what people want. If I had to bet on who'd be living in Hollywood in thirty years time – Me or Johnny Rotten – I know where I'd put my money!!!'

CREME BRULEE WILL SING WITH ROY NORTH AND OZZY THE OWL ON GET IT TOGETHER, THIS FRIDAY AT 4.15, ITV.

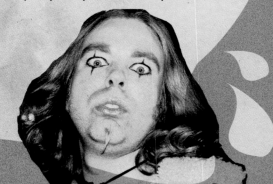

The MAGPIE Appeal

Murgatroyd

YES!!! IT'S THAT TIME OF YEAR AGAIN! FOLLOWING THE SUCCESS OF THE LAST MAGPIE APPEAL, SUSAN, TONY AND MICK ARE THIS WEEK SET TO LAUNCH A NEW FUND-RAISING PROJECT. LOOK-IN'S FIONA FLAPS VISITED TEDDINGTON LOCK TO FIND OUT WHY THIS YEAR'S APPEAL IS SO VERY DIFFERENT.

Finding your way to Teddington Lock studios is hard at the best of times, particularly when you're as drunk as I was. But it's even more difficult when you can't see. And that's the theme of this year's Magpie appeal. I asked regular presenter Susan Stranks to explain. At first she attempted to do this via popular arachnid glove puppets Itsy and Bitsy. After half an hour of high-pitched squeaks and low quacks, I begged her to return to conventional speech. Irritated, she complied.

'After the success of last year's 'Tractor's for the Damned' appeal,' says Susan, 'we thought we'd turn our attention closer to home.'
'I was driving home to my flat in the revolving restaurant of the Post Office Tower,' continues dark-eyed, delicate-lipped beauty Tony Bastable when – BANG! – I knocked something over. Next morning when I went back to look, it turned out to be a stray guide dog.'

'It even had its harness on which was protruding from its shattered ribcage, the lead drenched in blood,' concludes curly-topped newcomer Mick Robertson cheerfully.

It was then that the Magpie team became aware of a growing problem on the streets of Britain.
'It's those cunts at Blue Peter,' opines Susan. 'Their appeals have been so successful, that there are too many guide dogs to go around.'
'We've tried shooting them,' explains RSPCA chief and semi-pro wrestler Mick McManus, 'but because of selective breeding and the intensive training program, they are impervious to bullets. The only way to kill them is to stove in their heads with silver-topped canes.'

'So we thought if you can't beat them, join them,' comments Tony wryly. 'Instead of our usual crass and vulgar demand that you just send us your cash, we thought we'd try a bit of BBC philanthropy.'

'They're so fucking pious, don't you think Fiona?' says Susan. 'And completely without dignity. Noakes with his arse out after the Cresta Run incident, Judd snivelling through the ship-to-ship transfer, even Purves weeping publicly over his precious alsation. Please.'

But what exactly is the Magpie appeal aiming to do? Well it's a bold new enterprise.

1964

When Daleks invaded Earth, Christopher Trace launched the first Blue Peter appeal to repel the mutant invaders and London was saved.

1968

When starvation endangered Canada, Blue Peter launched their Save Canada appeal. Over a thousand metric tonnes of gas were donated by eager viewers.

BLIND MEN FOR THE DOGS

In a simple operation doctors can make any sighted person as blind as a bat. Just send in a milk bottle top together with the name of anyone you think should have their eyes put out, and they'll be matched up with one of the thousands of poor guide dogs now roaming the streets.

Mick concludes:

'I'm sure we all know someone we'd happily have blinded, either with a syringe or scalpel, or just a blunt stick. And it's all in a good cause.'

Here at Look-in we'd love to give a dog a blind man, but can Magpie really live up to those great Blue Peter appeals of the past?

1971

Britain panicked when top scientists discovered that GMT had developed a leak. Seconds were ebbing away at a rate of minutes per hour. Valerie Singleton's ground-breaking Stitch in Time appeal encouraged viewers to send in their spare minutes and wasted time.

1975

In order to raise money for Birmingham's first Life Boat, Blue Peter encouraged eager viewers to send in their piss, shit and rags. Over six million pounds was raised.

FREE!!!

with this week's poptastic

Creme Brulee Flexidisc

VOODOO LADY
by Creme Brulee

Ju ju hey hey
Voodoo Lady
Don't mean maybe
Black Magic Chile

The clock struck thirteen
And I was searching
For that midnight woman
of my darkest dreams.
She looked straight through me
Her spells undo me
My voodoo lady
Sweet witchcraft maid

CHORUS
Voodoo lady
Voodoo lady
I go goo
When you do voodoo

Then she smiled
Oh so sweetly
Thrilled me like a

Dennis Wheatley
She's got hexes
like no one has
But Baron Samedi warned me
Don't mess with that voodoo

CHORUS
Voodoo lady
Voodoo lady
I go goo
When you do voodoo

Ju ju hey hey
Don't mean maybe
Voodoo Lady
And the chills you gave me
I beseech you
From Satan save me
No one knows the secret of
The black magic box of my...

...Voodoo Lady
Don't mean maybe
Ju ju hey hey
Black Magic Chile

I have been doing lots of finding these days. This is
becas Edward had to go away to fight in another war. He
came back from the war last night. He won! Hee heeheehee
hee heeh ee hhee hhee hhee.

Edward has been given some medals for bravery in the war.
He had lots of little medals called pesetas, and one big
medal, which he hangs around his neck, like a big straw
hat!

Edward said he had a
quiet war. I asked him
why his skin
had turned brown,
and he said that
he had been
tortured. But when
he was putting on
his nightshirt, I
seed that they did
not burn his tail
or cut-back.

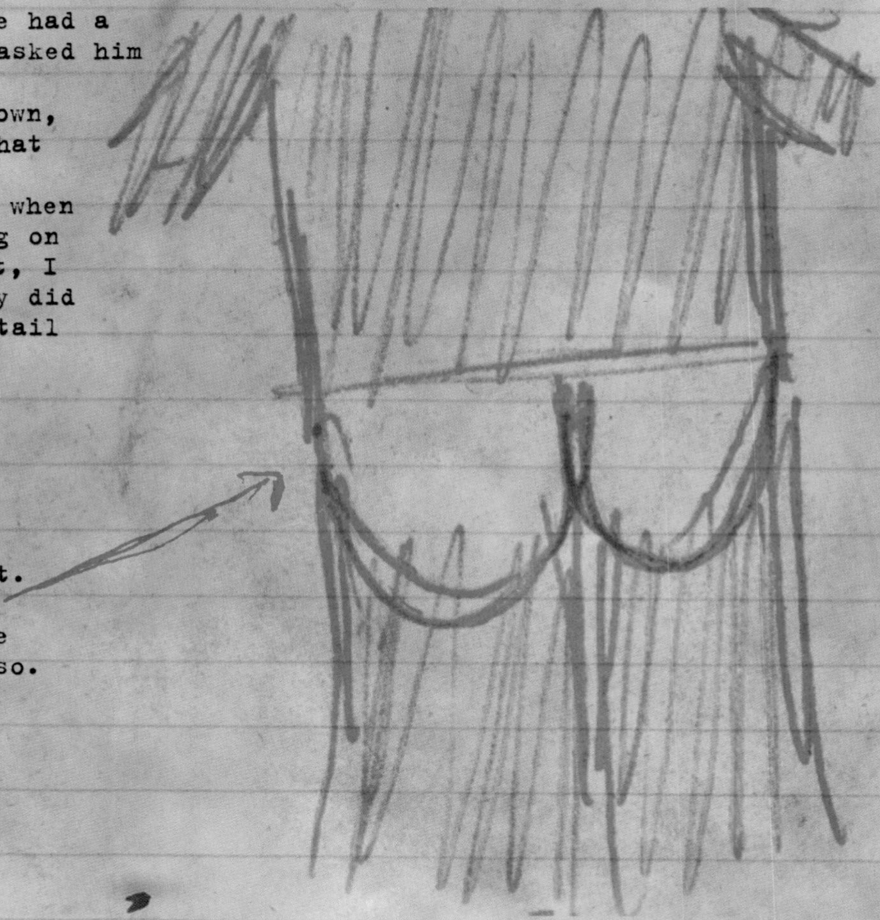

I ate the rest.
Poor Edward.
They must have
tortured him so.

This is a piece of Edward's skin which I peeled off in the night.

Here is a mirror baby of another soldier, which I found in my den. He is wearing the same uniform as Edward. He was in the Catalogue division. Maybe they were friends? I will put it in my book and see if Edward recognises him.

CLEVER Trebles

HENRY'S HOWLERS!

Greetings film fans! I have chose this week 4 vids which get my special 'W' certificate for being the most weariest films around. They are in no particular order of weariness, they are all just pig-shite boring. Avoid!

NEW

A CRY IN THE DARK

The idea behind this film is decent: a giant wolf is killing all the world's babies. However a quick look at the blurb on the back reveals two facts that should set the alarm bells ringing. 1: Made in Australia and 2: Starring Meryl Streep. The only good film to come out of Australia is 'Rawhead Rex' (a killer pig). Streep cannot make a good film. She is plagued by Oscars. This performance features a good black wig but the film is flawed because you do not see any killings. Give me the original – 'An American Werewolf in London' any day.

THE KILLING OF SISTER GEORGE

Save your money. There is no killing.

THE ENGLISH PATIENT

A film which is, basically, about sand. There is some enjoyment to be had in pausing it to look at the burnt face, but otherwise this is an overlong weepy where the main characters would rather talk to each other than kill each other. A disappointment for Ray Fines after the stunning 'Strange Day'.

MR HOLLAND'S OPUS

What is an opus? We thought it was a bumhole, and this might be a bluey for shitdicks. Him off 'Jaws' goes from the olden days to nowadays teaching music. Pure shit.

ALLY'S A-LIST!

Hello fellow Vid Vaulters! After all that bab, it is my pleasure to recommend some of the greatest films of all times. All these films were so good they went straight to video. Almost as good as Scanners when his head blows up. Enjoy!

CANNIBAL HOLOCAUST

Go to any video library and look in the Classics section, and in between 'Brief Encounter' and 'Casablanca' you would expect to find the 'Cannibal' trilogy – '...Holocaust', '...Ferox' and '...Apocalypse'. But no – these films are denied us. We, however, know Pigsy, and he's got them all on pirate. No acting between the killings, there is literally no story to these films. The effects alone should have scooped a Bafta. A must-see.

NEW

THE ISLAND

Possibly the most frightening film ever made. You will shit yourself. A Caine classic. (See 'The Hand').

RESERVOIR DOGS

What can we say that hasn't already been said? Whoever thought a man called Quentin could write and direct such a classic movie. (Though shame on you Mr Tarantino for not showing the ear come off! Pandering to the Oscar jury perhaps?) Anyway, spin it on past the first fifteen and enjoy – brainy but bloody, bloody good.

THE HAND

Before Oliver Stone met Kevin Kosta, he was quite a good director. Caine gives yet another brilliant video performance as a man whose hand gets chopped off. The killings do get a bit weary (all Strangles), but at least you see the hand come off (14 minutes in).

HENRY & ALLY'S VIDEO FINDER

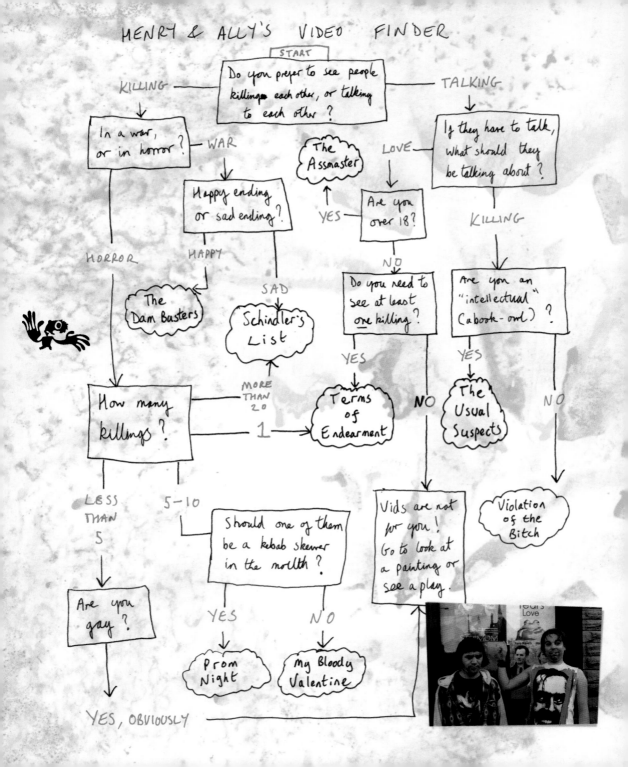

START

Do you prefer to see people killing each other, or talking to each other?

KILLING

In a war, or in horror?

WAR

Happy ending or sad ending?

HORROR

HAPPY

The Dam Busters

SAD

Schindler's List

MORE THAN 20

How many killings?

1

LESS THAN 5

5—10

Are you gay?

YES, OBVIOUSLY

Should one of them be a kebab skewer in the mouth?

YES

Prom Night

NO

My Bloody Valentine

The Assmaster

LOVE

YES

Are you over 18?

NO

Do you need to see at least one killing?

YES

Terms of Endearment

NO

TALKING

If they have to talk, what should they be talking about?

KILLING

Are you an "intellectual" (a book-owl)?

YES

The Usual Suspects

NO

Violation of the Bitch

Vids are not for you! Go to look at a painting or see a play.

Royston Vasey Chronicle

incorporating the **High Reporter**

18 HIGH STREET WEST, ROYSTON VASEY, RV1 5SF
Advertising: 0016 2010209 Editorial: 0016 0034917 E-mail: localnews@localpeople.co.uk

INSIDE

"YOU MA WIFE NOW, DAVE!"

WIN PANDEMONIUM CARNIVAL TICKETS

PAPA LAZAROU See Page 61

INSIDE

WIN COMPETITION WINNERS **DAFFY DADS** See Page 61

WOLVES DID IT!

by GEORGE PILLSON

• The three businessmen at the press conference. Tipps (centre) kept others calm 'with a few slaps and rabbit punches'.

A ROUTINE BUSINESS trip turned into a nightmare for three local plastics salesmen as they got lost on their way to their annual conference. In an emotional Press Conference yesterday afternoon, Geoff Tipps (40) told how he called on his Army training to survive the ordeal and care for his wounded employees, trainees Mike Harris and Brian Morgan.

The three businessmen, from Royston Vasey Plastic Injection Mouldings Ltd., were due to attend a three day conference at Shrigley Hall near Panties. But after an altercation with a minicab driver, they found themselves having to make their own way on foot.

"She was in a right foul mood," says Tipps of their taxi driver Barbara Dixon, "Kept saying he was 'on'. When I politely asked him what she meant, he just e x p l o d e d ."

Dixon, who courted controversy earlier in the year when she entered the Miss Royston Vasey competition and won (beating magistrate's wife Eunice Evans into second place), claims she was being sexually harassed by the burly Tipps.

"As a woman driving a cab in these remote areas, you're vulnerable. I know these lads from way back, and they're good lads. God, we used to play rugby together on Sunday afternoons. But on this day, they went a bit too far."

Dixon admitted ejecting the trio somewhere on the Salamander Pass between Panties and Royston Vasey, where they waited for three hours before setting off on foot.

"We tried hitching a lift, but three big fellas with suitcases...no b*****d would stop. We sent Brian out on his own, while me and Mike hid behind some sheep, but still no-one stopped."

Realising that it would be quicker to head for their hotel rather than turn back, the businessmen pressed on , in some way

"IT WAS ON 'GO WITH NOAKES', IT JUST STAYED WITH ME."

WOLVES DID IT!

From Page 1

• A wolf, like the one Tipps saw.

using Tipps' watch as a compass. "It was on 'Go With Noakes', it just stayed with me. But I can't explain how it works. I think the second hand was too fast. Anyway, we got lost."

Having arrived at the river Girl, Morgan and Harris began to cry with frustration, and were all for turning back. Tipps, however, called on his experiences with the Territorial Army to fashion a raft from twigs, heather, a bin-bag and shoe-laces.

"It sank", recalls Tipps. "Halfway to the other bank, Mike had a panic attack. I've seen this sort of thing before, if you're not used to this kind of situation you lose your head and start screaming and shouting. I tried to calm him down with a few slaps and rabbit punches, but he wouldn't keep still. We capsized."

Tipps dragged Harris to safety, then risked his own life to return for Morgan, who, being weak, had gashed his leg whilst scrambling to safety. It was then that they were

attacked by a creature described by Tipps as "a cross between a wolf and a crocodile."

"Looking back, it must have been a wolf, but I'm trying to explain why it was near the water. I don't care if no-one believes me, just ask Brian."

Morgan, who has yet to appear in public since the attack, issued this statement via close friend Katie. "Wolves did it. Ask Geoff."

Harris, who has no memory of his terrifying ordeal, was the first to be attacked.

"I'd just given Mike mouth to mouth", said Tipps, "and laid him out on the bank in the recovery position – face down with the hands tied securely behind the back. Then I heard Brian screaming 'My leg, my leg' or something, so I didn't think, I just dived straight back in.

"As I was pulling Brian's leg out of this metal spring, I saw out of the corner of my eye a black shape. It was wolflike, and it had Mike in its mouth. It

• Tipps at the scene:"Wolves did it" he claimed.

carried him away and tried to bury him."

When challenged during the Press Conference by Police animal expert Les Powell that it would be impossible for a wolf to carry off a human, Tipps erupted "it happened in Australia!"

Tipps, who can only urinate whilst sitting down due to a traumatic incident during childhood, then beat the wolf severely with a big stick. "The wolf was crouched near Mike's head,

so if there are any head wounds on Mike that look like I did them, then that'll be why.

"I just kept hitting and hitting. The wolf bit at me but I was too quick for it. The TA's prepare you for such attacks and I am light on my feet so I was able to avoid its lunges."

Asked how many creatures joined in the attack, Tipps replied "One. No, two. One or two."

Tipps' story, which was described by police as "beyond belief" was given further credence today following reported sightings of a similar creature on the moors above Royston Vasey.

Farmer Jed Tinsell reports hearing a strange howling noise "like a stuck pig" and has seen many of his sheep destroyed by what is becoming known locally as The Beast Of Royston Vasey.

"You can't blame me for the sheep. I really didn't do them!" Tipps explained. The investigation continues.

Dear Bernice...

...If you need the advice of a sympathetic friend, the Reverend Bernice Woodall has all the answers.

 **Star Letter**

WHIFFS OF PISS

Dear Bernice

I have a friend who smells of wee. Once before she slept at my house and weed the bed. I don't know whether to be her friend or not. Please help.
A Confused Five Fan

Bernice replies...
I can understand your concern pet. There might be many reasons for this behaviour but the answer to your question is 'no, do not be her friend'. She's got to learn that she can't go through life pissing in other people's beds. It's just rudeness.

TUMMY TROUBLE

Dear Bernice

Please could you help me? I'm scared of my own belly button. I feel ill about it and keep thinking I could never have a baby because of the cord. My naval is filthy but I can't touch it to clean it. Please help.
A Depressed Girl

Bernice replies...
Totally fucked up.

BYE BYE BUNNY

Dear Bernice

My rabbit Wiggles has got a runny eye. He is eight months old and lives with two guinea pigs. What should I do?
Ruth Wynn, Blacksnatch

THE ABYSS

Dear Bernice

When I was a child, life was perfect. My parents loved me, I was pretty and I had friends. Now I'm fifteen everything seems to have gone downhill. I'm spotty. My hair is lank and greasy. I'm taller than boys and they make fun of me. What am I to do?
Eve Barre, Spent

Bernice replies...
Don't get too worked up with adolescent angst because no matter how bad you think things are now it just gets worse and worse. Oh and once you get to forty then it really goes fast. I just look in the mirror now and an old woman looks back at me and I don't know who she is. Just have fun because you've no idea...

Bernice replies...
Now I'm not an expert, in fact I don't like animals, they scare me. But it sounds as if Wiggles is very ill and is going to die.
I hope you don't get it.

MY SPECIAL HELPLINE

If you need advice through a difficult or troubled time, my recorded messages are here to help.

• THERE'S NOTHING WRONG WITH VISITING P R O S T I T U T E S
0906 5812616

• YOU'RE FAR TOO FAT, LARDY. GET ON A DIET NOW. I DON'T CARE IF YOU'RE ONLY NINE
0906 5812327

• SO WHAT IF HE'S DEAD. GET OVER IT S I S T E R .
0906 5812333

If you would like to contact Bernice about any problems you might be experiencing, write to her here, at the Chronicle. The sender of the most distressing letter wins a £5 book token.

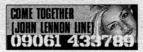

KETTLE OF COCKS

POLICE WERE SHOCKED to find a kettle full of human penises in a derelict house on the Redhawk estate. "This beats the belt of nipples we found last year!" joked PC Jerry Allen.

MONKEY BUSINESS FOR DOG CINEMA

LOCAL ENTREPRENEUR KENNY Harris — owner of Royston Vasey's famous Dog Cinema has gone 'ape'!

• First in the queue? Kenny's hoping for simian success at the Dog Cinema

AFTER THE SUCCESS of Kenny's experimental Pig Weekend he's seriously considering a simian film-festival to take place early next year.

'We showed Babe, Babe 2: A Pig In The City, A Private Function and Charlotte's Web. The punters loved it. They really enjoyed 'pigging' out. It got me thinking about all the other animals — except cats — that I could do seasons of. You know, maybe I was missing out on a goldmine here.' But what should come first? After toying with the idea of a Dolphin day — 'I were going to show Mike Nichols' Day of the Dolphin with George C. Scott, but I couldn't find any other dolphin films. I did consider making it a cetatcean weekend, you know showing it with Free Willy and Star Trek 4: The Voyage Home, but it didn't have the unity that pleases me.'

Undeterred Kenny hit upon another idea that had him 'swinging from the trees'

with joy.

'I were thinking what's the most popular animal in the movies after dogs? It's got to be monkeys.' The result: Kenny Harris' Monkey Fortnight which begins in the spring. 'I'm very excited about it,' enthuses Kenny. 'I've been on to all the distributors and I've already confirmations on Every Which Way But Loose and its even better sequel Any Which Way You Can. It's 80% on Romero's Monkeyshines, and I've got my own 16 mill copy of Congo so that's a definite. If I could just get Dunston Checks In then I'd be happy.'

The best news of all Kenny saves till last.

'I don't want people to get too excited but you know 'Boy' from the Johnny Weismuller Tarzan films, he might be flying over from Hollywood to open the season. I've written to him and asked anyway.'

Well, we cry a hearty 'ungawa' and hope the new venture 'apes' the success of Kenny's last venture — the one about pigs.

Daffy Dads Competition!!!

Another batch of paintings and drawings from the runners-up in last month's competition. £2 book tokens are on their way.

'My Dad can float and wee', by Zoe Lassiter, age 9

My Daddy is 'Mrs Punch' by Sean Yoffe, age 10.

'Funny Daddy' by Ellen Carpenter, age 4

'Toady Daddy' by Chloe and Radclyffe Denton, age 8

'Dirty Daddy' by Nigel Whitlock, age 40

Daddy's poo! →

Watch out for more competitions next issue kids!

Felch –

||||

Armando

~~||||~~ |

Goddle

||

Lovelips

~~||||~~ ~~||||~~

Royston Vasey

||

PAPA LAZAROU'S

★★★★ ★★★★

PANDEMONIUM CARNIVAL

THE WINDERMERE GUEST HOUSE

26 Hog Row, Royston Vasey, RV1 7JX

'The Fantasy Bureau'

Dear Friend,

Well, another three months gone by already! It seems only yesterday that I was on my hands and knees, face buried in the carpet, picking up those blooming pine needles after another Christmas here at the Windermere. I'm always telling Sunny we should be content with an artificial tree but as you know she likes her own way!

It seems our **Fantasy Bureau** goes from strength to strength. We now have **over 12 couples** interested in pushing the boundaries of married life in a consensual and loving environment. If you choose to join us for the next of our quarterly gatherings we can guarantee you a 'swingin' time, with all your needs catered for, including **full English or continental breakfast**, buffet lunch, light snacks, high tea and a no holds barred bout of communal intimacy if you're feeling 'randy'.

As well as being able to offer you en-suite facilities with moorland views, tea and coffee making facilities (nothing like **'jump leads'** to get you going first thing!) and complimentary shrewsbury fruit biscuit, the Windermere also provides a 'library' of marital aids for the modern couple. These include **two Real Feel Double Dongs, a Clit Stim, a Dr Johnson's Mr Realistic and just in from the US of A, gentlemen, the Slik-Lips Oro-Exciter complete with vibrating anal prong.**

'Having a swingin' time' at... The Windermere Hotel

(If, however, you prefer a nice quiet night in, can I recommend our compendium of board games, and my very own collection of Alistair MacLean classics including Fear is the Key, Puppet on a Chain and two Guns of Navarone.)

My good lady wife Sunny will of course be on hand for the duration of your stay. She is a trained **silver service waitress** and commis-chef who will take great pleasure in conjuring up all manner of fine English fare, and also an enthusiastic fellatrix, skilled in all aspects of restraint, bi-scenarios and role-play.

(Whilst on the latter subject there was an amusing incident a few months ago. A fellah called Chris turned up on our doorstep dressed as **Bilbo Baggins** or some such thing, wanting to know if he could vanquish 'the evil Smaug' in our rockery! I was going to call the police until I realised there had been a terrible misunderstanding viz the use of the words 'fantasy' and 'role-play'!)

The climax of your stay as always will be the Saturday night revels that take place in the Wordsworth lounge, where my wife Sunny enjoys **entertaining as many gentlemen as she can accommodate.** Previous guests will testify as to how she throws herself into these proceedings with gusto.

Of course there are those who at my time of life would like nothing more than to spend their weekends in front of the tellybox ticking off the lottery numbers, then after a pleasant conversation over a light meal perhaps the latest Frances Durbridge mystery at the Theatre Royal or the most recent action movie at the flicks. Not me!

The watchword here at the Windermere is **fun and laughter.** How often have I watched Sunny rocking back and forth on a stranger's hips shrieking again and again as she is transported to the heights of ecstasy, whilst I sit back shaking my head, the tears rolling down my face.

Come and join us, if you want.

Regards

Alvin + Sunny♡

Alvin and Sunny Steele.

Herr lipp **TOUR**S
----

see Englant by the back passages

GUTeN MOrgEN KINDER AND WILKOMMen INS EngLAND!
(Hi, welcome to England).

    I am happy to enjoy you to this exchange visit to the lovely town of Royston Vasey, which is going to be a real good treat for all of us. The purpose of this pomplet is to procure you with an infantry of all the exciting activities we have planned for you, and to give you a lick of what Royston Vasey may be able to offer. If any of the boys feel me to lack understatement, then wave your pink pomplet in the atmosphere and I will happily take you in my German mouth! Alles klar? Gut, alles klar.

ROYSTON VASEY AND DUISBURG

The first thing you will notice of Royston Vasey is the sign 'Welcome to Royston Vasey'. You will see that she is a town and that she is twinned in Germany with Duisburg. This engagement dates back to 1977 when both towns came equal-last in the Swiss edition of Jeux Sans Frontiers. I myself was a member of the Duisburg assembly, my task being to wet the Chefs and pull them off. It was very slimy, but a real good treat. So the marriage was born, and since then we have welcomed each other on exchange almost manually, if not bi.

DAY 1

The coach will leave the Schule at 08:15, stopping **ONLY ONCE** at the Hundkino for kinder from the Schwanmühleweg. From thence the drive will pass down into Holland via Aachen, then across into France, picking up the hovercat at Dieppe which will transfer you to Dover **by 03.40 UK time**. This is where I will meet you, having taken the plane direct. If you have any problems, Big Helmut should point you in the right direction.

DAY 2

We arrive in the lovely town of Royston Vasey in time to make our own tour, before meeting the kinder from St. Mark's. It is important that you beware the differencist in culture that England will offer you. English toilets are much dissimilar to our German ones. If you have never attended an English toilet before, there are a few surprises in them I must tell you of. Per example, there is no shelf for the examinations! But the pee wee is the same as you. Alles klar.

When we arrive at St. Mark's, you must mate with your palpens and start admiring them. Helmut and I will empty the luggage, which you must collect before you expire: **I DO NOT WANT TO BE LEFT HOLDING SOME BOY'S SACK.** I will be staying with the English teacher Bobby Smart, and I will want to get my head down as soon as possible.

So settle in and gut schlafen!

DAY 3

After a typical 'full English breakfast' (eggs, sausages, cauliflowers, tomatoe juice, plum jam, milk and toadstools) we will recommence at the Schule and take a trip to Royston Vasey Heritage. This is a museum into which all of Royston Vasey can be assumed. The technologies of this museum are enough to wet your lips, as special lights and sound effect transport us back in time, from the Middle Ages up to today. You and your partner can see some mannquins in fancy dress as a lute plays on tape and a man's voice shouts through 800 years of history. A real good treat, hmmm?

The afternoon is free for private activities — I have some in mind for myself — then we should congratulate at **Flick Flacks**, where a disco will be in operation until 10 o'clock, **so get frigging!**

DAY 4

The trip to the **Roundabout Zoo** has had to have been cancelled, due to all the animals having disappeared.

DAY 5

I will be leading a tramp into the fields and hoping to top myself at Peggy Mount, which is the tallest hill in Royston Vasey (last one up is a queen!). After some comely photo-opportunities, I will be making love to the boys by offering traditional English games to sample, such as **British Bullfrogs and Blind Man's Puff**. I have played with boys for many years now and each of them says this is amongst the highlife of the exchange.

(I should explain. British Bullfrogs is an English version of our Küssfang, where the boys must run at each other without being held. If you do catch a boy, then his mate must kiss your lips to escape him. In Blind Man's Puff, I will be the Puff and you must blind my eyes. Then I shall creep among you and try to catch somebody. When I have him, I must feel who you are and name the name of my captain. Per example... Dieter! Then Dieter becomes the Puff und so weiter, und so weiter.)

USEFUL ENGLISH PHRASES AND THEIR MEANINGS

Act the goat	To be silly, or worship the devil
Bummers are deaf	New expression. I have not heard it
Cool!	A real good treat
Down in the dumps	To have diarrhoea (Durchfall)
Exocet	A toy for fat ladies with short hair
Frigging	A disco dance where the fingers are bent like tiny hooks
Get stuffed/get stood on	Expressions of woe
Howzat!	A goal in cricket
In yer face	Safe sex
Jumble sale	Chain of fashion stores for hobos
King	A queen's boyfriend (the stone)
Lebkuchen	A German cake (not as nise as Duisburg cake!)
Making hay	Obscene word for sexual interplay
No way, Jose!	Yes
Oxo family	Similar to our Familie Soße, but the daughter is fat with round glasses
Piss off	To finish the last drip-drops from your toilet (the pee wee is the same as you, remember)
Queen	A ladyking (sponge)
Red rag to a bull	A lesbian's monthly (not a magazine)
Sod	A bad man who walks on grass
Tipsy	Bi
Up 'n' under	A lesbian's monthly (a magazine)
Vegan café	A smelly room full of people with bad breath
Wanker	One who makes his own hay
X-rated	A film which may feature a circlejerk (Kreisruck)
Yes	Kein Weg, Walter!
Zzzzzzzzz	We are bored with these phrases Herr Lipp, let's play games now. OK boys. You win!

DOGS' ARSES

£4.9

BOW WOW WOW!

CENTER SPREAD SPECIAL!
WEEING WONDERS

INSIDE

BITCHES ON HEAT
READERS DOGS

AUTUMN 1999   ISSUE 01

4 0012333   4 3454398

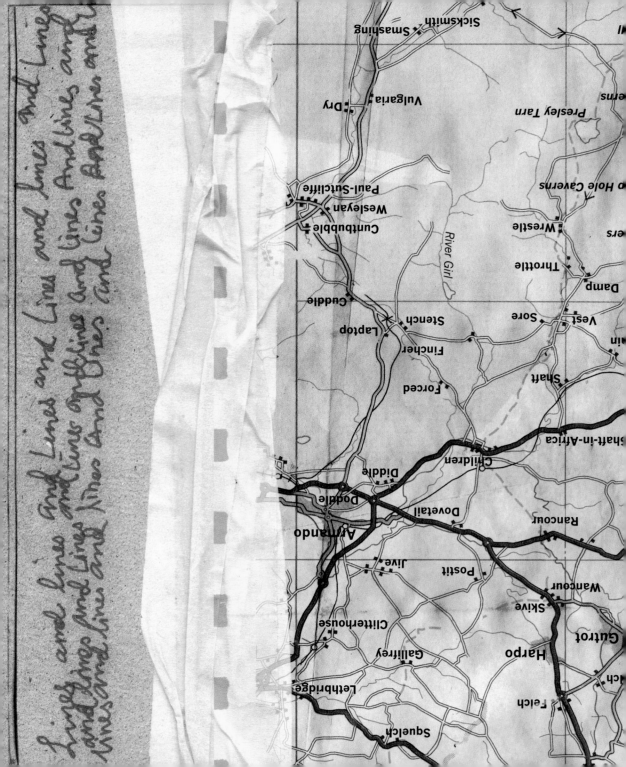

The Arts Council of Great Britain
14-16 Peter Street
London WC1 2XX
1st September, 1998

Dear Sir/Madam,

I enclose a first draft copy of my new play "North" as well as some promotional information about Legz Akimbo Theatre Company. If you are not interested in providing funding for my play, please return the manuscript in the envelope provided, as my printer is not working and this is the only copy of the text. My bank details for the grant are as follows. Account number 68973271 at the Nationwide in Rugby, sort code 44-82-40.

LATC was founded in 1988 by myself and my ex-wife Linda, now a lesbian. Our original aim was to set up a repertory company of exciting young actors who would explore vibrant new writing by Oliver Plimsoles. However, the small-minded petty bureaucracy of the Nottingham Council Arts & Parks Board forced us to consider a move down, to London and children's theatre.

Our first project was Classix Now!, a vibrant miniseason of pub and street theatre experiences which opened in Stratford, East London. The Supersonnet Rap Show had audiences captivated, and they were kept going throughout the 8 hour piece by glasses of mulled wine (Linda's recipe and her only involvement in the production) and my vibrant performance. I was eventually moved on by London Underground staff, but had developed such a "rapport" with the audience members that they both signed up to join the company that same day (a Friday). Legz Akimbo was born!

Other actors came and went. "The Three" now laugh about a certain spotty young upstart who "dried" in the middle of Turkey for One, a play about Christmas. He only lasted for two months out of his 13 month contract. His name: Stephen Thompkinson, star of TV's Drop the Donkey and Hamish Macbeth. He doesn't mention that in interviews!?!

So the company went from strength to strength, with tours going to Wales, Scotland, Finland and almost America. Would it have made a difference to your grants committee if Thompkinson had still been around? Certainly would have helped me stage the vibrant, adult-themed Man Feeding Cats, a play about me. Just because it's not aimed at kids or crippled black gypsies doesn't mean it's not a valid piece of work. What's fifty pounds to someone like him - he's booked up with offers of work until 2005 and I know that for a FACT.

Anyway, Yours in anticipation,

Oliver Plimsoles

OLIVER PLIMSOLES

Writer, Director, Producer, Actor (lead)

ISSUES THROUGH THEATRE

L EARNING STUFF IS BORING, ESPECIALLY IN A SCHOOL ENVIRONMENT! ✗

E DUCATION IS FOR THE CLASSROOM, NOT THE HALL OR GYM!! ✗

G IVE ME SPACE INVADERS OR A DISCO OVER THEATRE ANY DAY!!! ✗

Z ZZZZZ - PLAYS ARE LIKE ASSEMBLIES, WAKE ME UP WHEN IT'S OVER!!!! ✗

KEY
*SEE SKILLS AND CROSSBONES, A PLAY ABOUT CAREER OPTIONS
**EXCEPT FOR POB-POB AND THE MILK MACHINE, A PLAY FOR BABIES. POB-POB MERCHANDISE AVAILABLE.
***ASK FOR DETAILS ABOUT SILENT ISSUES, A PLAY WITHOUT WORDS; ALSO, PLAY ON WORDS, A PLAY FOR DEAF KIDS.
****ALL LATC ACTORS ARE FAMILIAR WITH STANDARD RESTRAINING TECHNIQUES SUCH AS 'DECKING' AND 'JIBBING'.

AUDIENCE PARTICIPATION GETS YOUNG MINDS WORKING, ESPECIALLY WHEN SIR OR MISS IS MADE TO WALK THE PLANK!* ✔

KIDS ARE BABY GOATS! WE TREAT OUR YOUNG AUDIENCE MEMBERS IN EXACTLY THE SAME WAY WE TREAT THEIR TEACHERS.** ✔

IDEALLY YOU WILL PROVIDE COFFEE AND CAKES UPON OUR ARRIVAL. A SEPARATE DRESSING ROOM WILL BE REQUIRED FOR OLIVER PLIMSOLES. ✔

MIME IS A UNIVERSAL LANGUAGE. LATC HAVE PERFORMED TO KIDS IN THREE DIFFERENT COUNTRIES AROUND THE WORLD.*** ✔

BRINGING THEATRE INTO THE CLASSROOM CAN DRAW DIFFICULT KIDS OUT OF THEMSELVES, REVEALING A WHOLE NEW SIDE TO THEM.**** ✔

OLIVER PLIMSOLES CAN PROMISE YOU AN AMAZING EDUCATIONAL THEATRE EXPERIENCE, PLUS AN AFTERNOON OFF NORMAL LESSONS. ✔

PAST PRODUCTIONS

OLIVER PLIMSOLES HAS WRITTEN AND PRODUCED SOME 30 ISSUE-BASED PLAYS FOR YOUNG MINDS OF ALL AGES. THE FOLLOWING ARE SOME OF THE MOST WELL-KNOWN.

EVERYBODY OUT! (HOMOSEXUALITY); OFF-LICENCE TO KILL (TEENAGE DRINKING); WHITE CHOCOLATE (RACISM); CEREAL KILLERS: SMACK, CRACK AND POT (DRUGS: FRINGE FIRST EDINBURGH FESTIVAL 1992); THERE'S A HOLE IN MY OZONE, DEAR LIZA, DEAR LIZA (ENVIRONMENT); PETER PICKED MY POCKET MONEY (BULLYING); CALLIPER CALYPSO (DISABILITY/RACE); SEEDLESS GRAPES (FRUIT MACHINE ADDICTION); KIDZKIDZ (TEENAGE PREGNANCY); ONE, JEW, BUCKLE MY SHOE (RELIGION); HEROES IN HELMETS (GAYS IN THE MILITARY); STINKY MATTRESS (BEDWETTING).

LEGZ AKIMBO

PUT YOURSELF INTO A CHILD

IN ADDITION TO THESE KIDZSHOWZ, LATC ALSO OFFERS INSIGHTFUL AND VIBRANT PRODUCTIONS OF CLASSIC BOOKS AND PLAYS FROM THE GCSE CURRICULUM AIMED AT OLDER STUDENTS (BUT CAN BE LIVENED UP FOR THE TOTS - ASK FOR DETAILS ABOUT WILLPOWER, BRECHTASTIC AND ARTAUD & THE WHEELIES). USING JUST THREE ACTORS, MINIMAL PROPS AND YOUNG IMAGINATIONS, LET LEGZ AKIMBO PAINT WORDPICTURES IN YOUR HALL OR GYM (IF HEATED), TRANSFORMING STUFFY PLAYS AND NOVELS FROM PAGE TO STAGE.

WHO'S WHO IN LATC?

OLIVER PLIMSOLES

OLLIE SET UP LEGZ AKIMBO SHORTLY AFTER LEAVING UNIVERSITY. WHILST A STUDENT, HE WAS HEAVILY INVOLVED WITH THE DRAMA SOC, PLAYING EVERYTHING FROM A LITTLE BOY TO AN OLD MAN. OLLIE'S FIRST PLAY AS A WRITER WAS A TWO-HANDER FOR HIMSELF AND BI-WIFE LINDA ENTITLED BLOOD ORANGES, WHICH TOURED BRITISH CANALS ON THE U.K.'S FIRST BARGESTAGE (MAYBE THIS IS WHERE RODNEY BEWES GOT THE IDEA FOR HIS THREE MEN IN A BOAT ?). AFTER A YEAR OF REP AT MUSSELLBOROUGH, WHERE HE PLAYED BARDOLPH IN MERRY WIVES AND THE HENRYS, OLLIE RETURNED TO HIS FIRST LOVE: WRITING PLAYS FOR HIMSELF TO STAR IN. IT WAS WHILST WATCHING A 1987 ROGER COOK PROGRAMME ABOUT 'THE HOT-DOG WARS' THAT OLLIE HIT UPON THE IDEA OF INTRODUCING ISSUES INTO HIS WRITING. AFTER HIS FIRST COMPANY, ISSUEZ-IN-MOTION, FOLDED DUE TO PATHETIC IGNORANCE, OLLIE BOUNCED BACK WITH LEGZ AKIMBO. THE REST, AS THEY SAY, IS HISTORY. BE PART OF IT (BOOK NOW).

DAVE PARKES

DAVE'S FIRST ACTING JOB WAS PLAYING DR. POTTSON IN THE ADVENTURES OF SMELLSOCK PHONES FOR FINLAND-BASED COMPANY BLACK SHEEP THEATRE. HE LATER TOURED EAST GERMANY WITH TWO OTHER BLACK SHEEPERS AS DUNCAN / FLEANCE / PORTER / LADY MACDUFF / BANQUO / SERVANT / 3RD MURDERER / 3RD WITCH / DRIVER / ASM-SWING IN A 9 MONTH TOUR OF MACBETH. OTHER THEATRE INCLUDES A DRAMATISATION OF POLLY PUT THE KETTLE ON FOR HICKORY DICKORY DOCK TC. A KEEN MUSICIAN, DAVE DROVE THE VAN FOR THE ALL-GIRL BRASS BAND THE FALLOPIAN TUBAS. HE HAS APPEARED IN EVERY SINGLE LEGZ AKIMBO THEATRE PRODUCTION.

PHILL PROCTOR

TRAINED AT BRETTON HALL COLLEGE (BA HONS. THEATRE ARTS). THEATRE INCLUDES PICKCHOOSE IN THE GOODLY MISTRESS (BRETTON HALL); SINGING RAVEN / TIT / BATTERY HEN 4 IN THE BIRDS '90 - AFTER ARISTOPHANES (BRETTON HALL); PORGY IN PORGY AND BESS (BRETTON HALL). SOLO SHOWS AS WRITER/PERFORMER INCLUDE NOTHING TO DECLARE: OSCAR & I (BRETTON HALL & BEDLAM THEATRE, EDINBURGH); THE MONOCHROME RAINBOW: GARLAND & I (ETCETERA THEATRE, LONDON); PINK TARDIS: AM I WHO I AM? (STUDIO THEATRE, MOLD); GREEN CARNATIONS, RED RIBBONS: I'M A GAY ACTOR (SLEEP WITH ME) (NATIONAL TOUR). TV & FILMS INCLUDE FAIR DEAL? CUSTOMER CARE & SERVICE: VOL. 3 (TRAINING VIDEO FOR NETTO SUPERMARKET); BURNT MAN IN LONDON'S BURNING (ITV. EPISODE 38 - OLD FLAMES. DIRECTOR: PAUL BRACEWELL.). VHS SHOWREEL AVAILABLE UPON REQUEST.

LINDA PLIMSOLES

AFTER LEAVING HER HUSBAND TO GO AND LIVE WITH A FEMALE GEOFF CAPES, LINDA IS NOW NO LONGER INVOLVED WITH THEATRE OR THIS COMPANY IN ANY WAY WHATSOEVER. BLAH BLAH BLAH THINK OF SOMETHING BEFORE SENDING THIS TO THE PRINTERS BLAH BLAHBLAHBLAHBLAH FUCK YOU LINDA, SEE HOW I CAN DO ALL MY OWN ADMIN ALL YOU EVER WERE WAS SOME KIND OF SECRETARY TO ME I'M NOT SURPRISED YOU NEVER HAD AN ORGASM MY FRIDGE IS MORE EROTIC THAN YOU I MISS YOU COME BACK BLAH BLAH.

"north"
by OLIVER PLIMSOLES

ACT 1. SCENE 1.

The front room of the GREYFOLK's terraced house, somewhere in the North. A dog sits on the sofa, metaphorically, but also literally, licking its wounds. (If this is not possible, then a plastic canary can be seen, trapped in a cage. Either way, an issue should be portrayed by part of the set.)

DAD GREYFOLK is asleep in the armchair, the Racing Post or The Sun open on his lap (Important: he is NOT a stereotype, he must look real.) SKRIKE GREYFOLK, the son, stands before the "mirror" (ie. the audience) adjusting his tie and putting Brylcreem in his hair (sponsorship possibilities?) in an exaggerated-ly naturalistic style - see Berkoff for the moves.

SKRIKE: Hair! Shave! Tie!

HAIRSHAVETIE!

HAAIIRR! SHEEAAVVEE! TIIEEE!

KILL! KILL! KILL! KILL! KILL! Arghhhhhhhhhhhhhhhhhh!

Silence. A shattering silence. DAD speaks.

DAD: Where ya goin'?

SKRIKE: Mind your own stink!

DAD: Mind your stink!

SKRIKE: Mind yours! Stink, stinking skint, skint as I am. There's poetry in our voices, but it dunt come out right. Poverty is poetry with an extra 'V'. Only nowt rhymes wi' it!

SKRIKE takes a penny from his pocket (maybe exaggerated in size) and throws it to the floor. As if from nowhere, MA enters and scrabbles around on the floor for the penny. MA is wearing a polka dot head scarf and pinny, and is either obese or anorexic, or any other issues. WARNING: if the stage is raked, the penny may roll into the orchestra pit. A good character actress may be able to do something with this. Pam Ferris, for example.

MA: Can I do a speech? Can I? I will then.

Taps. Big taps on me bath, rusting away.

DAD: Like the country?

MA: Country? Cunt-tree more like, like the taps in Ma's big bath.

I want the taps to work.

I want me man to work.

I want work for me man, but there in't none.

Not here in't North.

DAD: Not here in't North.

SKRIKE: Not here in't NOOORRRTT

TUBBS PLAY

by Tubbs Tattsyrup

TUBBS is in the local shop counting the precious things of the shop.

TUBBS: One, two, five, twelvety, six, ten, none, four...

EDWARD enters the shop.

EDWARD: Hello, my love. What are you doing, I love you.

TUBBS: I love you.

EDWARD: David loves you.

TUBBS: I love David.

EDWARD: You look nice.

TUBBS: Thankyou. Can we go to London?

EDWARD: Yes.

THE END.

THE SHULL MONTY

Is this Another play?
Lots of hel-mets!

Where They Are Hidden

Ten Acre Field

A fine pasture-land. Stands fallow every third season. Primarily of use for turnips and other root crops. Its guardian – ostensibly a thing of cloth and straw – is young Andrew Ward.

I saw him first at the Cash and Carry. Very polite he was in his fine suit as he helped Gracie fill her bags. "Always build your corners, Mrs. Tinsel," he winked. "Heavy produce first, perishables on top." He would soon pay for this familiarity though I kept quiet at the time.

I found him on her one afternoon. I was just back from the plough. He was sheened in sweat. There was no doubt. They'd been a-swiving all the live-long day. I pulled her off with a hook and he tried to fight but I brought my gun up under his chin. It all went dark for him.

When he woke his feet were cased in concrete and I had dressed him in some of my old clothes. "You're a fine sight Andrew Ward," says I. "Not so handsome now you've shat your nice grey suit are you? Is he Grace?" She was quiet. I got him in the barrow and took him out to ten acre. I'd been up half the night making a bag out of oakum. I planted him, just like a tree and pulled the bag tight over his screaming head ha, ha, ha.

Duffer's Piece

Moderate grazing land. Verdant in Spring. Subsidence leads to flooding in the lower portion. Its guardian is old Jack Marks.

I was following Gracie by now. She was not to be trusted. When she said she needed some stamps I knew what she was talking of. Old Jack Marks was the postmaster. They do say he was quite a catch in his day and he was handsome still, though 78. The old grey fox, I thought.

He made sure Grace was head of the queue. Then he served her well. Wetting his fingers as he counted out her pension. Tearing off her postal order with treacherous old claws. Giving her a nice shiny wallet for her car tax. I would have a nice wallet for him soon, ha, ha.

Now the kiddies trick or treating on Hallowe'en do not know what they laugh at when they cycle past him. He won't be stamping my Grace's book again. Old Jack o'lantern with a pumpkin for a head.

The Yard

Cockles. Some concrete. A crazy paved path to the old water pump. Its guardian is Giles. He was our son.

By now, no-one was to be trusted. Giles was at home all day. It was the holiday. He was a pretty boy. He had his mother's looks. Oh he liked it when she gave him bacon and eggs. "Thanks mum" I heard him say. The swine. But I held my peace until it was time. Oh yes I'd been watching. I asked him to come and help me with the milking. I'd been watchful of the herd ever since my prize cow went missing and Giles thought I was just being circumspect. Little did the black villain know that what was in my heart was revenge, revenge.

I clamped the milking machine to his little mouth and milked the air right out of him. Those eyes would not lock with his mother's ever again as I stuffed him into the water pump. His bones cracked like dry old twigs, yes they did.

The Breakfast Table

A fine old table. Early 20th century. Polished oak, with well turned legs. Its guardian is Grace, herself.

I watched her. She polished it, she wiped it. She put knives and forks on it. Her red rose mouth would drool as she ate over it. She loved it too much. What choice did I have?

Enough was enough under my own roof. She was missing the boy and anxious to be gone. "I'll go to the police Jed Tinsel. I know where you belong," she cried. I boiled a hundred eggs and made her eat them one by one. Her belly swelled then she fell ill. I stitched her mouth up with string and sat her down at her beloved table. She can watch it forever now.

DATE	PERSON'S MISSING AND DESCRIPTION	DETAILS
15/2	ANDREW WARD – M, 32. Retail worker. Last seen leaving ~~Bisons~~ Hammonds to head off to Tinsell's farm.	–
11/9	KATHERINE BRADLEY – F, 74 or 76. Blue dressing-gown, long grey hair. Thinks she's a cat. Answers to the name 'Nana'. Can be coaxed with milk.	BODY FOUN ON CHURCH ROOF – ID. PENDING
7/11	MARTIN LEE – M, 28. Rambler. "Lovely curly hair" distinctive red boots	–
7/11	PC BOBBY WOODWARD – M, 42. Uniformed police officer.	Helmet found 13/12 charred.
19/11	CLASS 2B – M/F 8-9 year olds; last seen Stump Hole Cavern.	Guide questioned check previous record?
17/1	Mary Hobbs (F). Housewife. 44. Husband claims she ran away with a black man.	⎫ SAME DAY ?
17/1	ANNIE RAINES – (F) 82. LAST SEEN AT TRAVELLING CARNIVAL; 50+ WITNESSES CLAIM SHE ONLY WANTED TO BE WITH HUSBAND – WHO DIED LAST YEAR. PRESUME SUICIDE.	⎭
20/2	[ROSS GAINES – M, 34. Glasses, side parting. Works at Orel House. Milkbottles building up outside house. Holiday? Friends/Family?]	✳ Found 28/2 see CAMPBELL-JONES file for details.
13/3	JUSTIN SMART – M, 15. Schoolboy, last seen with friends at Flick Flacks – claimed he was going to a party. Gone to Germany ?	· c.f. Derby & Reading special brands. similar MO ?

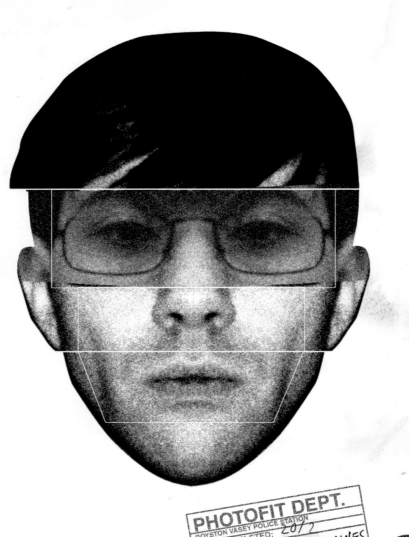

PHOTOFIT DEPT.

ROYSTON VASEY POLICE STATION

DATE COMPLETED: 20/2

SUBJECT NAME/DETAILS:
ROSS GAINES

INVESTIGATING OFFICER:
INSPEC COX

CASE CLOSED

FILE NO: 1128/2

P.O.P. ESTATES

Estate Agents-Surveyors-Intimidation
0016 444 4244 (Gary will take a message)

RENTALS

Dunraven House, Christie Road.
£750 ppm*
Stunning apartment with four walls and door. Minutes from pavement. There is also a shop not far away.
Fully fitted lightbulbs and switches.

The Copper-Beeches, Langley Drive £330ppm**
Charming, detached, highly characterful and well upholstered chair. Fabulous views of fireplace. Close to MFI unit and temperamental black and white portable. A bargain!

Eaton Place, Tumbledown £670ppm***

Prestigious, sophisticated bachelor apartment. Large and roomy hole where window used to be. South facing. Stinks of cat's piss.

*(NB ppm means pounds per Monday, not month as some have tried to argue.)
**(NB ppm can also mean pounds per minute and does in this case, alright.)
***(NB occasionally can mean 'pay Pop's mortgage' as in this case.)

ASSURED SHORTHOLD TENANCY AGREEMENT

TAKE NOTICE that the tenancy granted under this agreement is an ASSURED SHORTHOLD TENANCY under *part 1 of the Housing Act 1988*, amended by ωηεββττϖαγδφ - hereafter call me Pop, Gary. The landlord may require access to your property, chattels, effects, goods, correspondence, larder, motor vehicle, fuel, monies, good-will and woman, upon giving the required notice (three minutes).

THIS AGREEMENT is made on the date stated in paragraph A of the Schedule (hereinafter referred to as 'the Contract' which you DO NOT BREAK – not without consequence) BETWEEN the Landlord named in paragraph B of the Contract of the one part and the Tenant – hereafter my servant, lackey, retainer, plaything, subject and child.

WHEREBY IT IS AGREED as follows:

1. The Rent shall be paid monthly in advance on the 1st day of each month during the Tenancy by Pop's preferred method (put credit cards/Switch/Delta in envelope wrapped in piece of paper with PIN number on it and I will get out cash Gary).

2. The Tenant agrees to pay Rent on said day or on any other day deemed by Pop, alright? It is my lawyers you see. They are *Wampyr.* We have a saying in the old country: "*Εετοπανφητωενλκηγρυγφλννβξ,ηφοπικμχξμζ,ξλ.ξμνχϖφ*" which means "pay the money, pay it now, pay it to Pop".

3. The Tenant undertakes to pay electricity, gas, telephone, water and the entirety of Pop's bills as well as the tenants own.

4. The Tenant agrees to pay and indemnify Council Tax, Landlord's Income Tax, Window Tax, Corner Tax, Beard Tax (these last three, Gary, are directly payable to the Landlord ie: me, Pop. You may not have heard of them but do not worry I will sort it all out for you).

5. The Tenant consents that the Landlord may take any images whilst the Tenant is in possession of the property (including when his woman is alone) and exploit in any and every medium including all electronic and digital formats (videos, super 8, DVD – I know this man with a pressing plant in Grozny). Tenants also agree to license their images for display on the website hereinafter known as www.garyandlynnedoitlive.com.

6. If the Premises – or any of the Landlord's other premises – should be destroyed by fire, flood or men with a grudge, the Tenant consents to rebuild the property brick by brick, with his bare hands, and to live in a crawlspace with a box on his head for as long as it so do please.

P.O.P. ESTATES

Estate Agents-Surveyors-Intimidation
0016 444 4244 (Gary will take a message)

TO BUY

"Le Chambre de Mort", Backbottoms £49,000

Excellent opportunity for redevelopment. Large, tiled living/dining area. Roomy cold storage facilities. A number of impressive original features including trays of surgical instruments and steel tables with holes in them for flushing guts down.

"The Wall", Glove Grove, £26,000
Ideal for first time buyer, this solid, practical and well-located wall comes complete with bricks and mortar. Can be leaned against with coat draped across for shelter.
Things live in the Ivy.

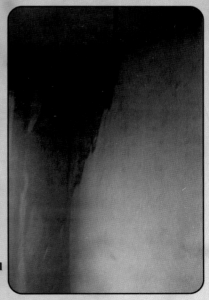

"The Penny Hang", Banacek, £17,000
Upstairs room with rope slung from one wall to the other. You can hang off it at night.

THE CURSE OF KARRIT POOR.

THE CURSE OF KARRIT POOR

Being the Reminiscences of "DR EDMUND CHINNERY R.C.V.S."

I. – A MYSTERIOUS SUMMONS

S I write, the new century is scarcely begun. It is the age of invention, of the electric light, the motor car and the gentlemen's combination shoe and sock. The old queen is dead. It seems impertinent, of course, to refer to him as such, but Dr Timothy Majolica was always the 'old queen' to us in our student days. And it was he who led directly to my involvement in the narrative which I am about to unfold; a story so fantastic that it might seem to have sprung from the ravings of some brain-fevered Eastern mystic. Or a twat.

In the winter of 18– I was still a young man recently matriculated from the Royal College of Veterinary Surgeons and looking to establish myself in practice. At that time I was sharing rooms with an old college friend, Shankly Jackpot, a bohemian soul who was at that time earning a living as a wrestler or female impersonator – I could never remember which. My degree was a good one and yet I confess to finding myself disappointed at the paucity of advertised situations. I'd even considered employment as resident vet at the Happy Gluepot – a retirement home for shire horses when I received one of my former tutor's enigmatic telegrams.

"Come and see me tomorrow if you like. If you've not got too much on. About three would be alright. Well anytime really. Or next week. I'm free.

Cheers. TM."

"Not quite as enigmatic as usual," commented Jackpot archly.

Unperturbed I took the train to Cambridge and soon found myself back amongst the cloisters in which I had been so recently and happily ensconced.

It was a glorious day and the winter sun dazzled over the slate roofs of the colleges like spit. When I arrived Dr Majolica was saying goodbye to one of the boys from the Poor School. He would regularly invite these boys to his rooms for tea, and private Greek tuition. As I entered he gave me a ready smile and patted his latest charge on the head, sending him back to his classroom with a twist of sherbet, a copy of Euclid and a whispered "Tell anyone about this and I'll fucking kill you".

"HE HAD ERRED IN EVERY RESPECT"

Puzzled by this last remark I was on the point of saying something when Dr Majolica threw himself down onto his sofa and began to fill his pipe from the toe end of the old pair of tights in which he kept his strongest tobacco. He gazed at me with the intensity which my fellows and I had come to know so well.

"You have put on a little weight Chinnery," he remarked with a smile. I shook my head. "Yes I fancy you have. I also observe that you travelled from town today in a four wheeler, that your driver was a dwarf lascar with odd shoes, not long discharged from the Welsh Fusiliers, and that you sat opposite a bachelor typist from Altrincham who wore a greasy hat and had recently anointed his thinning hair with chocolate. You ate a full breakfast of eggs, bacon, sausages and paper which you washed down with a thimbleful of blood." He sucked on his pipe and clapped his hands together.

"I trust nothing has escaped me."

I could only shake my head in wonder, for he had erred in every respect.

"I have in fact lost over two stones in weight sir," said I, "after contracting the trots over summer. I came to Cambridge by train and sat alone. I can't stand eggs and certainly wouldn't—"

"Yes, alright, alright," he said testily, his face falling. Hastily he refilled his pipe and made a show of tidying some of the special photographic plates which were his hobby. I reflected once again that although my tutor was a first rate veterinarian, as an analytical reasoner he was shit.

Over tea he told me of a vacancy which he had heard in the firm of Boothby, Canker and Purblind.

"Mr Boothby is an elderly gentleman," Majolica explained, "and in poor health. But I have some little acquaintance with the other partners. If you like I can put in a good word for you." I was naturally thrilled and accepted Dr Majolica's kind offer, only demurring at his suggestion that I might want to come in to his darkroom and look at some pictures of "naughty people".

"And where is this practice?" I asked. My old mentor smiled thinly.

"It is in the North Country," he said at last. "A charming little place called Royston Vasey."

II. – THE MAN ON THE TRAIN

THE day on which I travelled north was a cold one and I had several times to wipe away a rime of frost from the carriage window. The train huffed and puffed like a pig with asthma, meandering over a bleak landscape of skeletal trees and frozen waterways. Occasionally I spotted a sheep, or a huddle of cows in the lower end of the field and I smiled to myself, thinking how soon I would have my arm thrust up them, probing for tumours or expediting difficult pregnancies.

The train had just pulled out of yet another lonely station, when the door of my compartment was drawn aside. I looked up and saw an extraordinary figure. Swarthy and with his left ear pierced for rings, he sported a battered top hat and eye patch. With his barrel chest and sinewy neck he could have been taken for a natural athlete were it not for the complete absence of arms and legs.

"'Ow do," he called brightly as he was thrown bodily into the carriage by the station master. He thanked the man for his trouble and then shuffled past my legs. With an effort he managed to wriggle his way on to the opposite seat and rolled himself a cigarette using only his long leathery tongue.

"Edmund Chinnery," I said by way of introduction.

"I am Kinky John," he said solemnly. "Might I have something for you?" So saying, he bit open his coat revealing rows and rows of vegetables which were attached to the lining.

I frowned. Kinky John laughed.

"I expect these things is a bit saucy for you, with your towny ways."

"What do you mean?" I replied with some asperity. He fondled the nearest vegetable with unhealthy tenderness.

"The leek. The potato. The red cabbage and his white cousin. These are things that a fine gentleman such as yourself feigns disinterest in".

"I'm sorry?"

"Shut away in your ivory tower with your London ways. Pretending you is so respectable, when you and your kind brood on such things as these. And go a visiting your special places to satisfy these 'forbidden' desires."

" 'DESIRES FOR VEGETABLES?' I QUERIED"

"Desires for vegetables?" I queried, for his tone had nettled me. Kinky John nodded.

"Some call 'em that, aye." He lapsed into silence.

I coughed and drew my great-coat tighter around me. "Well, I hope that your 'country ways' may be more familiar to me soon Kinky John. I'm on my way to Royston Vasey –"

The freakish fellow paused from stroking his cheek against the bulb of a Spanish onion.

"Vasey," he gasped. "Why?"

"I am to be interviewed for the position of assistant veterinary surgeon in the firm of Boothby, Canker and Purblind". Kinky John looked at me for a long moment and then gently manoeuvred the onion back into his coat.

"And tell me sir," he murmured, "with whom is your appointment to be kept?"

"It is with Mr Purblind," I replied. "His younger partner is away in town. And I gather Mr Boothby is not a well man."

My strange companion nodded. "No. That he ain't."

Again we fell silent. A moment later the train drew into another station.

"This is me, Blacktup," announced Kinky John, rolling off the upholstery and struggling, slug-like, towards the door. "Royston Vasey's just one more stop."

I thanked him for his companionship but there was more to come. He lent down towards his lapel and managed to drag something from his pocket with his teeth. He tossed it into the air and I caught it deftly.

"Take this," he said.

I examined the object. "A beetroot?"

He nodded. "The nights are awful cold and lonely." I slipped the vegetable into my waistcoat then fell back astonished as Kinky John launched himself at me, landing in my lap like a monkey, or a man who might as well have been a sock.

"For the love of God, Dr Chinnery," he gasped. "Stay away from Royston Vasey! Get the first train back to Chicago –"

"London."

"Whatever. Get away from here and don't think no more of Boothby, Canker and Purblind!" So saying he tumbled from my lap and out of the train.

It can easily be imagined that Kinky John's warning had left me with a feeling of deep unease. It took me fully five minutes to realise that it was caused by the beetroot sticking into my tummy.

III. – AN APPOINTMENT IN ROYSTON VASEY

ROYSTON Vasey appeared much as I imagined it: a small, fairly prosperous settlement with the usual quota of shops and civic buildings. A memorial on the main street commemorated those townsfolk who had fallen in war. On close inspection however I was surprised to see that over one hundred and fifty Vaseyites had apparently perished in the American war of independence as a consequence of catching the wrong boat on a day trip to the Isle of Man. I soon found the practice of Boothby, Canker and Purblind and was made welcome by the latter, a pleasant-seeming individual with a wooden eye, who looked over my credentials with evident satisfaction. The upshot was I was offered the position at once and I thanked him profusely.

"There is only one thing," said Mr Purblind at length. "Mr Boothby is an invalid. He never stirs from his bed from dawn till dusk, save to go for a wee. He occupies the last room on the third floor. The door is green baize, studded with sequins. You cannot miss it."

"You wish me to visit him then?"

Purblind's expression darkened. "On no account," he almost hissed. His voice softened and he removed his wooden eye, polishing it on his jumper. "Mr Boothby is a very sick man. And the slightest disturbance is abhorrent to him. Any attempt to break this instruction will render you liable to immediate dismissal. Do I make myself clear?"

"Perfectly."

Mr Purblind smiled. "Capital. I think we shall get along very well."

That night I slept fitfully. I was awoken between two and three in the morning by a terrible sound. At first I took it to be the wailing of a cat outside the casement, but with a shudder I realised that it came from within the house. In fact it must have come from the room above my own. With a thrill of horror I knew that it was the room with the green baize door. And the sequins. I held the beetroot tight. The sound came again. A fearful caterw-

"HE NEVER STIRS FROM HIS BED FROM DAWN TILL DUSK, SAVE TO GO FOR A WEE."

-auling as though a soul were in dreadful torment. I thought of Mr Purblind's warning. But how could I ignore this poor old man's distress? With a heavy heart I lit a candle and made my way out onto the landing.

I crept across the bare boards and swiftly made my way across the stairs. In the flaring light of the candle I saw the green baize door at the end of the gloomy corridor, sequins twinkling. The door was slightly ajar and a thin sliver of light was peeking through from the room beyond. With a final glance around me I pushed it open and went inside.

IV. – THE TERRIBLE TALE OF MAGNUS BOOTHBY

ON a bed almost lost in a miasma of pillows lay what I assumed to be Mr Boothby. He was a tiny, etiolated, shrivelled up thing, more like something I would discard from the dissecting room, than a man. He still was a man of course but sort of horrible like a baby lamb in its birth sac. Or an old pear. Suddenly his eyes sprang open. Dark tiny eyes they were, like two flies in rice pudding. He beckoned to me and gingerly I advanced.

"Mr Boothby," I stammered? He inclined his head a fraction. His hair and beard were wispy and white, like semen in the bath.

"I am Magnus Boothby," he croaked. "Are you the new boy?"

I introduced myself and the ancient creature nodded slowly. "Did they tell you you mustn't come in here?"

"Indeed sir, but you sounded in such distress."

"Distress!" Boothby let out a high-pitched laugh. "The term does not do justice to my condition," he said, his voice as dry as paper. "I am accursed."

I sat down on the edge of the bed. What on earth could he mean?

"You would not think it to look at me now Dr Chinnery, but I was once a young and handsome fellow."

"When?" I asked.

"Well a long time ago."

I shrugged. "Well we all have to get old." He shook his head impatiently.

"I know that. I'm trying to say that I'm old beyond my years. My life has been blighted. Twisted out of shape by the forces of darkness."

"I see."

"Have you ever heard of Karrit Poor?" he asked.

"The cricketer?"

Boothby closed his eyes and sighed. "It is a province of India. I was stationed there at Roye Castle. As chief veterinary surgeon. I was much loved. My practice flourished, treating everything from the sacred cows to the memsah'bs' pampered dogs."

I nodded.

"Now the Maharajah of Karrit Poor had a favourite pet – a little monkey called Topov. I had often wondered if the Maharajah would favour me with a call. But none came. Not until that fateful afternoon. Oh woe!"

I calmed the old man down. He clasped my hand with his own. It was dry and gnarled like a twig. Or like the hand of a very, very old man.

"My only vice," continued Boothby with a whisper, "was drink. And I fear I was absolutely bladdered that day, for I had been celebrating the successful treatment of an outbreak of bovine veruccas in a sacred herd. The message came that Topov the monkey was very sick with a delicate condition which couldn't be described in writing and would the English veterinary sahib please honour the Maharajah with a consultation. I hastened from the castle to the palace and saw at once that it was indeed a matter of some delicacy. Topov was known to be a cheeky monkey with an overactive libido who enjoyed the simulation of coitus with almost anything that came to hand. On this occasion he found himself in a compromising position with the Maharajah's ornamental pencil sharpener – fashioned in the shape of a large ivory elephant. With utmost tact I assured the anxious Maharajah that the little fellow's 'little fellow' could be freed with the simple application of ordinary vaseline. I reached for the pot in my case, together with a spatula, and applied a circular smear of the substance around the root of Topov's genital cluster. Despite my inebriation I was pleased with my handiwork, as was the Maharajah, who promised me riches beyond my wildest dreams, a palace by the Ganges and the hand of his beautiful daughter, plus the rest of her if I was interested.

"But what was this? The little monkey was shrieking, clearly in agony. A plume of what looked like steam was issuing from the back end of the ivory elephant where it conjoined with the monkey's hips. I struggled to focus on the jar of ointment in my hand. What I saw made me blanch with fear. For it was not vaseline that I held, but sixteen ounces of Buller's Full Strength Bovine Verruca Acid which even as I read the label was eating its way through the root of Topov's unfortunate member.

"The poor creature pulled himself free and skittered pell mell across the floor, expiring in a steaming heap of simian anguish. The tripartite genital disjecta membrae flopped to the floor and the thud went as a dagger to my heart. The Maharajah stared at me".

Boothby let out an anguished howl. "Never have I seen such a look upon a human face!" he croaked. "Sometimes on a cow's and once on a gorilla's, yes, but this! The Maharajah swore he would be revenged. He picked up Topov's little jewels and, holding them aloft, he called upon his Gods".

At that, the old man opened the front of his nightshirt. For an instant I thought I understood why Mr Purblind had warned me not to go into his room, but then I noticed that around Boothby's neck was a small, shrivelled object. Like an amulet. Or a rabbit's foot. But most of all like the burnt off bollocks of an Indian monkey.

"Topov's parts!" I ejaculated.

Boothby nodded. "Touch them and see!"

I did not want to. I swear. But something seemed to compel me to touch the damned furry things. My fingers closed around them and at once I felt a strange sensation steal over me. I looked down at Boothby and to my unutterable horror I found that he was laughing.

"Free," he chortled. "Free at last!" I knew at once that something was terribly wrong.

"Free," I whispered hoarsely. "Free to do what?"

Boothby threw back the bedcovers and staggered back out onto the floorboards. Free to practise veterinary medicine! Free to pat a puppy on the head! Free to give a gerbil an enema with minimal risk!"

"I – I don't understand," I managed to say. Because I didn't. Understand.

At that moment the door opened and Purblind came in dressed in his pyjamas.

"It is over then Magnus?" he asked, grinning like a demon. "The curse is lifted?"

"Curse? What curse?" I all but screamed.

Boothby turned towards me cackling in triumph. "The Maharajah's curse. That any animal I touched would meet a dreadful end. A vile terrible curse. And, to be honest, absolute professional death for a vet."

"And I have lifted the curse?"

Purblind nodded. "By taking it upon yourself! For years we have waited. And then your old tutor told us about you, Chinnery. He said you were just the kind of well meaning imbecile who would fit in with our plans. Another vet has touched the monkey's bits! And now you - and all your descendants - will suffer the curse of Karrit Poor!"

"And I can move to Harrogate," cried Boothby. With which rather baffling comment he and Purblind left the room.

I was alone. Betrayed by my former friend and stitched up rotten by my new employers. I threw the dreadful cock and balls into the corner of the room and reached inside my nightshirt for Kinky John"s lucky beetroot. Amongst the roots I found a dead weevil. Of course I could have squashed it during my sleep. But I knew at once that its lifeless carcass told a different and more dreadful story...

TransPoses

SheMale Fashions

Hi girls!

Welcome to our brand new Autumn 1996 collection. Sick of sneaking into your wife's knicker drawer while she's at the Spar on a Saturday afternoon? Weary of being caught in a pair of Pretty Pollys and a too-tight basque when the gas man calls round? Here at TransPoses we give you all the time, space and pancake you need to bring out the Woman Within.

A TransPoses day is a day where dreams come true. First, pick a LadyLook from the brochure and check that we have it in stock. Then an ex-doctor will come and measure you up for your BreastFriends (if we don't have them in your size, a pair of football socks will be provided). Once you are dressed up, our ladies (real ones, not men in dresses) will pamper you and tell you it's not wrong.

Partners are welcome to join in the fun, perhaps choosing your make-up or shaving your back. A "fashion shoot" will then take place in our basement studio (we keep the negatives) and you will have time to chat with other TransPosers in the DannyLaRoom. Your magical day climaxes when you are wanked off by a builder in the ladies loos.

So c'mon Girls pick a lady and come to TransPoses, it's femtastic! (fantastic)

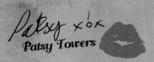

Patsy xox
Patsy Towers

This Autumn's SheMale model is the lovely Barbara, a pre-op mini cab driver from Royston Vasey. She is modelling four spectacular LadyLooks for your wardrobe.

"Thankyou TransPoses you've made me feel like a REAL WOMAN!"

Jean from Sorehole

*NB: All TransPoses models are women of mystery and their identities must remain secret.

* NB: all LadyLooks come with thick black choker to hide the telltale Adam's apple, and gloves to disguise them big hands

sizes
available from
12-50

Maud
"The Spinster"

George
"The Docker"

Clothes: Maud's tweed two-piece will get you in Miss Marple mode within seconds!
Make-Up: Thin lips, liver spots and light moustache/beard.
Hair: Grey with grips (hat optional).
Accessories: Pince-nez, ear trumpet, pipe, wheelchair, butterfly net, dentures.

Clothes: With George's jumble sale frock, knee-length boots and pink cardigan, people will really believe you're a big man who dresses up as a woman.
Make-Up: Mother Goose.
Hair: Wife's long curly 60's wig, found in back of wardrobe, or on a shop dummy.
Accessories: Tattoos, long red fingernails, far too much jewellery, stupid voice.

Look what I found!

I was just liing outside counting twinkles and I'd got to twelvety when all of a suddenly this piece of paper blowed into my face. At first I didnt like it. I thought, 'This cant be Edward becas Edward promised that he would take _me_ to London first, to see Les Mis.' Also the no-tail he is with looks like une salope (I dont know this word in English yet).

But then I realised! Edward has been looking for a no-tail to marry our son David in the attic. He must have thought that we would never find a nice local no-tail, so he went to London with the flashbox. Oh kind, considerate, thoughtful Edward!

Everything starts to make sense now. Edward hasn't been going away to buy supplies or fight in a war. No!!! He has been planning the wedding. And the supprise party isnt for my birthday, it is going to be a reception party!

Pamela Doove

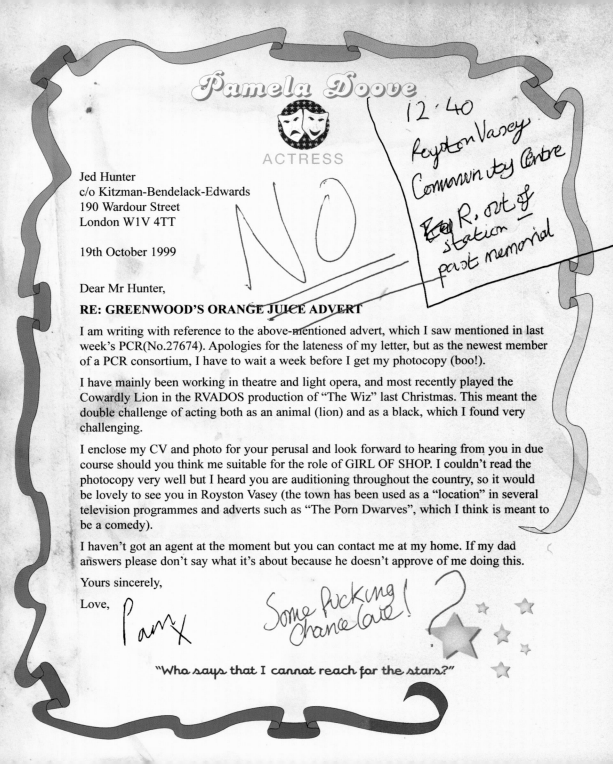

ACTRESS

Jed Hunter
c/o Kitzman-Bendelack-Edwards
190 Wardour Street
London W1V 4TT

19th October 1999

NO (handwritten)

*12.40
Royston Vasey
Community Centre

Eg R. out of
station —
past memorial* (handwritten)

Dear Mr Hunter,

RE: GREENWOOD'S ORANGE JUICE ADVERT

I am writing with reference to the above-mentioned advert, which I saw mentioned in last week's PCR(No.27674). Apologies for the lateness of my letter, but as the newest member of a PCR consortium, I have to wait a week before I get my photocopy (boo!).

I have mainly been working in theatre and light opera, and most recently played the Cowardly Lion in the RVADOS production of "The Wiz" last Christmas. This meant the double challenge of acting both as an animal (lion) and as a black, which I found very challenging.

I enclose my CV and photo for your perusal and look forward to hearing from you in due course should you think me suitable for the role of GIRL OF SHOP. I couldn't read the photocopy very well but I heard you are auditioning throughout the country, so it would be lovely to see you in Royston Vasey (the town has been used as a "location" in several television programmes and adverts such as "The Porn Dwarves", which I think is meant to be a comedy).

I haven't got an agent at the moment but you can contact me at my home. If my dad answers please don't say what it's about because he doesn't approve of me doing this.

Yours sincerely,

Love,

Pam x (handwritten signature)

Some fucking chance love! (handwritten)

"Who says that I cannot reach for the stars?"

Three views of Pam Doove

Happy ...

Sad ...

The Wiz!

SO YOU WANNA BE A STORE DETECTIVE?

Two Day Seminar With Christopher Frost.

I T I N E R A R Y

09.30am Arrive at Stuarts Commercial College. Greetings and coffee. (Bring change for machine).

09.35am Introduction: What do you think you're doing here?

look them in the EYES oo you mean business

This lecture will provide you with an introduction to the job of store detective. It is designed to weed out the jokers, straight out of college, who think this job is an easy option. T'ain't. We have a saying in the business: You can't hide a turd in a kitchen. If you are not serious about being a store detective, I'll smell you a mile away. Get out of my kitchen. Chalk you up.

PAUSE. Walk up and down look like you're thinking.

10.15am Case histories.

We will examine three incidents that have changed the course of store detection throughout history.

Case 1: These images were discovered etched into the caves near Chamonix, France. Do they represent the first recorded incidence of shoplifting? Was the culprit apprehended, and if so what was his excuse? Chalk him up?

Case 2: China 1956. Mother of seven, Xai-Yu Cheung, was apprehended leaving a market in Peking with a whole rolled up rice pancake in her windpipe. She was discovered when the stall owner asked her a simple arithmetical question, and she was unable to reply. The case made history when Cheung, defending herself, argued that because the pancake was partly digested it was no longer theft, simply "accidental consumption". She lost. Chalk her up.

Case 3: On a March afternoon in the early '90's, a gentleman shopper was politely asked to step to one side by one of our uniformed colleagues in a certain branch of a well known super-market chain, somewhere in the North of England. The "gentleman" was discovered to have a number of bottles of a well known brand of wine about his person; four bottles of which - it was revealed - had not been paid for. Chalk him up. The gentleman's name? Ah, that would be telling - but the fact that he was at the time a well loved and respected television personal-ity, ensured that the issue of SHOPLIFTING was brought back into the public consciousness for the first time since Cheung.

[handwritten, top right:] Do NOT TELL

12.00pm Lunch. The sandwiches provided are free. If you wish to make other arrangements you may do so, but our sandwiches are NOT to leave the premises. This is tantamount to shoplifting (although not illegal).

[handwritten:] Try not to make a big issue out of this. That fight was unnecessary.

12.30pm "The Excuses".

This is a bit of fun as I tend to find some individuals are often a bit giddy after their lunch half hour. We go round the room and laugh about the various excuses one might come across in a typical shoplifting incident. I'll give you a few of the classics to get the ball rolling:

• "Sorry I totally forgot! I've got the money here look. I don't mind paying now".

The ALL TIME classic. Any good store detective worth his salt will have heard this a hundred times and will know how to deal with it. On a more serious note, the second half of this excuse is tantamount to bribery. Be careful.

• "I thought this was a free promotion. I'll put it back then".

My response? "I thought you were a shoplifter, I'll put you down then. For a long time".

• "I am a kleptomaniac. I have a doctors certificate to prove it".

Basically this is a lie. I only understand part of the word. Maniac. Klepto? That must mean shoplifter. So what are we left with? A shoplifting maniac. Beware. But chalk him up.

13.00pm Whodunnit?

Look at the scene below: Who are you watching? Where are you watching? Who is the most likely to commit a crime. Answer: THEY ALL ARE. CHALK 'EM UP.

Now look again. Is that woman really pregnant or is it a bag of Little Imp barbecue coals, retail price £6.99? Chalk it up. Study the cripple. Could those crutches be hollow, filled with what? Fifty-seven items from the pick and mix, all pushed down. Retail price, and I'm going out on a limb here, much like him, £2.50? Chalk 'em up. Obvious one… what's in the pram? I doubt it's alive, unless it's a spider plant, retail price £4.75. Chalk it up. Look at their throats… big Adam's apples? Or Cadbury's Creme Eggs (remember Cheung). And finally our old friend Fatty. We know she's greedy and has a desire for things, just from the fatness of her. She's wearing a hat: that's two rump steaks, special offer £3.64, chalk 'em up. The coat with baggy sleeves, three Curly Wurlys and a white Toblerone, £1.12, chalk 'em up, and I dread to think where she's stuck her fish fingers. (Chalk 'em up.)

[handwritten: We had been to this. pick out — seemingly unimpressed]

14.30pm Practical On Site Field Trip.

This is an opportunity to watch the master in action. The training methods I use are based on the FBI's, which I saw on a documentary whilst I was in hospital waiting for my operation. I will walk you around my normal route at Binns or Hammonds as it is now known Superstore, and you will see me putting all of the above theory into practice. The on site observations will take place in and around the store at places of interest to your average lifter.

1) **The Cheese counter**. For some reason most people begrudge paying for cheese. Especially mild cheddar. We will regard the processed cheeses for 15 minutes.

2) **The Pick and mix.** Sure to have some activity. Usually some greedy little pig child sticking his hand in the cola bottles or pink shrimps. People tend to think casually helping themselves to a handful of chocolate raisins isn't stealing. IT IS. It's the same with grapes. (If we have time I will prove this.)

3) An unusual detour I like to make is to the public toilets provided in the store. I like to check the cubicles for any odd balls, and often I will check all the cisterns for hidden bottles of scotch; often what happens is first time lifters chicken out last minute and leave what they thought they'd steal in the toilets. Well it happened once anyway. I always check in case it has happened again.

4) I will make it my business to apprehend one malfeasant during this trip, be they guilty or otherwise, and allow each of you to interrogate the suspect in the tiny manager's office - the manager not the office, whilst I hide behind a screen. Do not look behind the screen at any time. Good luck.

Remember: shoplifters do not pay for their goods. We do. That makes me feel humiliated. Let's chalk 'em all up for good. GET 'EM!! !!!!!!!!!!!!!!!!!!!!!!!!!!!!!!!!

[handwritten: Do NOT explain this. You must not be drawn.]

Charity Shop Book for May 23rd, 1999

23/5/1999	1 (one) jigsaw depicting Stockholm Harbour (incomplete)	Mrs Krell (Sainsbury's bag)	50p
" " "	1 (one) cassette of music - "Tout Sweet: The Best of Crema Brulee [note:- top of cassette has been sellotaped over and 4 (four) episodes of "The Moral Maze" recorded from Radio 4 - that Merrill [!.]	Al (Threshers bag)	5p
" " " " "	3 (three) bags (plastic, clear) containing 8 (nine) pairs of ladies (dead) spectacles	Lady (came with own bag)	£1.00
"	2 (two) quality novels - good condition. "Lipstick and Lies" by Jacqueline de Grachy Galedin ; "Tropical Slut", by Rev. Bernice Woodall (soiled)	Barbara (Dixons bag)	20p
"	1 (one) board game - "Mousetrap" + "Escape From Colditz" combined in one box	Val Denton (2 (two) bags needed due to size of box !!!!..)	66p

[LUNCH]

" " "	1 (one) plastic dish stacker (beige with green bits) ; 5 (five) ex-army metal mugs (chipped) [note:- impossible to hold when containing any hot liquids]; 1 (one) kitchen bin (lidless) ; 3 (three) assorted cushions ; 1 (one) Trimphone in avocado green [444 4244]; 2 (two) paintings of blue/black women. [Came as a set of 3 (three), but Merrill sold one seperately - that Merrill]	Foreign gentleman (black bin bag)	£2.1
" " " "	1 (one) pen on a string [like "Swap Shop"]	M. Michaels (no bag requested:- bag refused !)	6p
" " "	4 (four) Beta-Max video films :- "Death Camp Vixen" "Die, Kim, Die" "Die, Kim, Die II: The Gift" "Bugchasers"	Two boys (long hair) (Burtons bag)	*1.
www	1202 (twelvetty) Precious things I like this book. The story is Exciting but it is Not believable that a shop would sell so many things / HEE HEE HEE	Tubbs (leather bag)	Free

0208 1344 229

Slim,
Tall,
Classy & Elegant

Aims to Please
19 yrs
34DD-22-32

Very Leggy

Hotel Visits

maismarcia@cjb.net

Edward is planning
a special supprise
party!!!

I know this becas
last night when I
needed to make some
petrol, I seed that
Edwards shoes were
still all tied up
(Edward never
untangles his shoes.
Naughty Edward!)
Anyway, when I lifted
them up, this mirror
baby fell out of the
left shoe.

To begin with I could not puzzle it out. Why would
Edward have such a mirror baby? Who is she? Is she
local? (she looks local, but I've never met her). Then I
realised — Edward is planning the reception, so he is
getting all my relatives together who I have never seed
befor!! This must be my cousin Anne or my nephew Robert.
Clever Edward.
I love him so much and he loves me.

I will not spoil the party tho, so I re-shoed the mirror
baby and i will never mention it and till the
"supprise"!!!

And we have found a lovely bride in BARBARA, and she'll be able to give us lots of little Tubbs and Edwards and the shop will carry on forever and ever and ever and tomorrow will be the happiest day of my Life and as I write this I can taste my EYES for the FIRST Time Ever.

Issued to
Jr Michael Sinclair

Aug 1692

BARLOW & STRAKER
L'SALEM'S   MAINE

TEMPTATIONS LTD

JUST OFF THE EDGEWARE ROAD....